The Making of C. S. Forester's

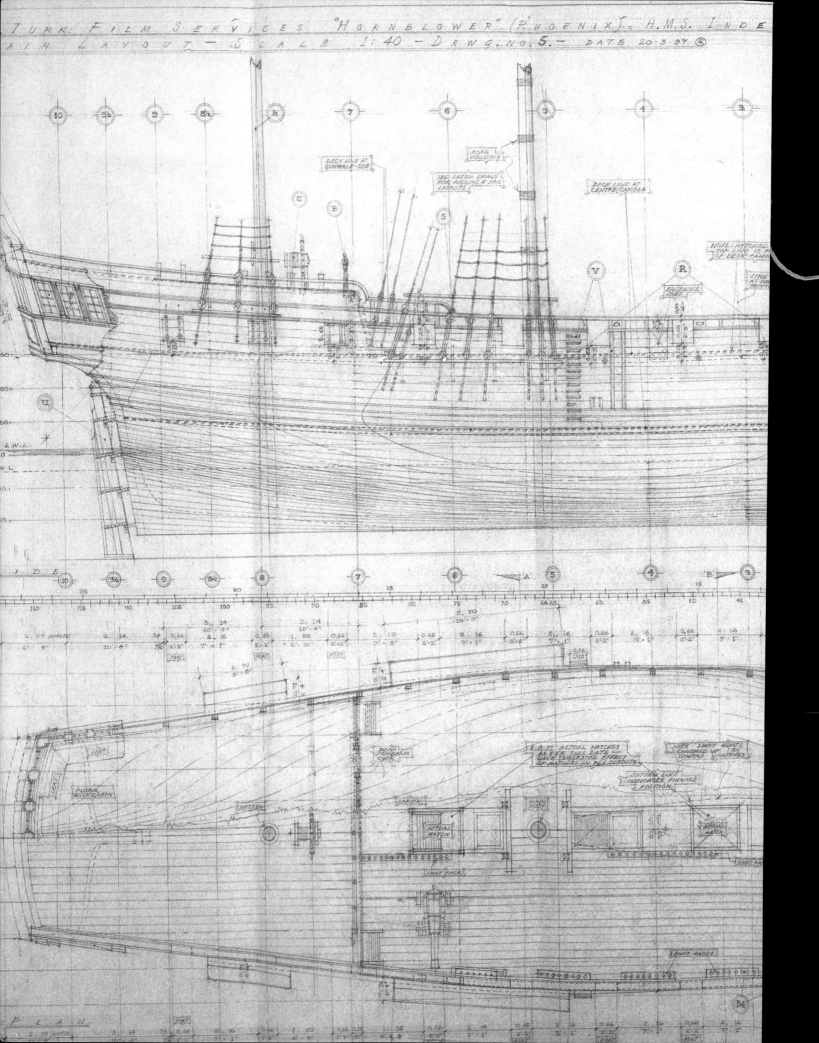

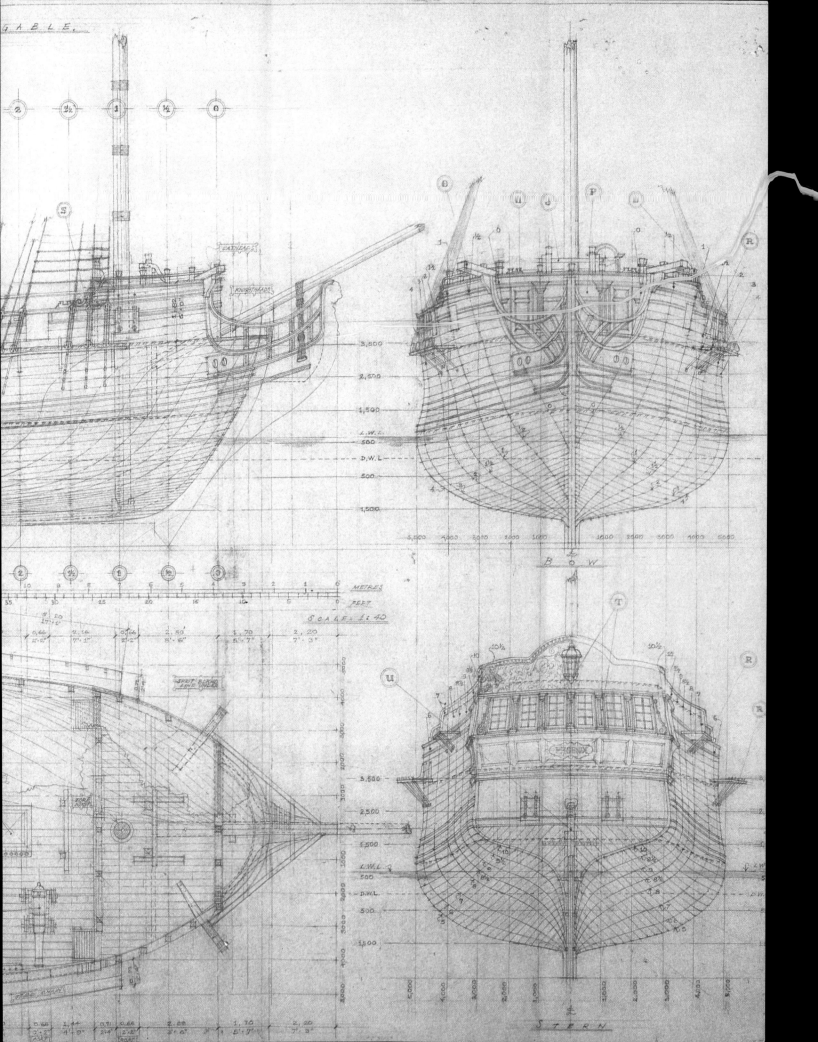

The Making of C. S. Forester's

HORATIO
HORNBLOWER

Tom McGregor

HarperEntertainment

A Division of HarperCollinsPublishers

Hornblower
CAST AND CREW

Ship's Company

Hornblower	Ioan Gruffudd
Captain Pellew	Robert Lindsay
Matthews	Paul Copley
Styles	Sean Gilder
Oldroyd	Simon Sherlock
Lieutenant Bracegirdle	Jonathan Coy
Midshipman Kennedy	Jamie Bamber
Master Bowles	Colin MacLachlan
Finch	Chris Barnes
Midshipman Cleveland	Frank Boyce

'The Even Chance'

Midshipman Simpson	Dorian Healy
Captain Keane	Michael Byrne
Lieutenant Eccleston	Robert Bathurst
Midshipman Clayton	Duncan Bell
Lieutenant Chadd	Roger May
Captain Forget	Vincent Grass
Midshipman Hether	Richard Lumsden
Dr Heppelwhite	Simon Markey
Lieutenant Chalk	Oliver Montgomery

'The Duchess and The Devil'

The Duchess	Cherie Lunghi
Hunter	Christopher Fulford
Don Massaredo	Ronald Pickup
Sir Hew Dalrymple	John Woodvine
Etienne de Vergesse	Jean Yves Berteloot
Spanish Lieutenant	Vincent Boluda
Collins	Ian Lindsay
Captain Joubert	Jolyon Baker
Stevens	Jason Hall

'The Examination for Lieutenant'

Captain Foster	Denis Lawson
Tapling	Ian McNeice
Bunting	Andrew Tiernan
Captain Hammond	Ian McElhinney
Steward	Rupert Holliday-Evans
H.M. Consul Duras	Peter Corey
Commander Morris	Simon Slater
Spanish Captain	Frank Rozelaar-Green
Clerkly Officer	Jonathan Aris

'The Frogs and The Lobsters'

Moncoutant	Antony Sher
Lord Edrington	Samuel West
Charette	John Shrapnel
Admiral Lord Hood	Peter Vaughan
Mariette	Estelle Skornik
Fauré	Jean Badin

Crew

Producer	Andrew Benson
Director	Andrew Grieve
Line Producer	Peter Richardson
Directors of Photography	Neve Cunningham
	Alec Curtis
Production Designers	Andrew Mollo
	Rob Harris
Costume Designer	John Mollo
Sound Recordists	Christian Wangler
	Rudi Buckle
Make-up Supervisors	Christine Allsopp
	Veyatie MacLeod
Film Editor	Keith Palmer

Originally published in the United Kingdom in 1998 by Boxtree,
an imprint of Macmillan Publishers Ltd.

THE MAKING OF C. S. FORESTER'S HORATIO HORNBLOWER by Tom McGregor.
Text copyright © 1998 by Meridian Broadcasting Ltd
Photographs © 1988 by Meridian Broadcasting Ltd.
Photography by Rod Ebdon and Peter Bolton
Photographs on pages 56, 68 and 74 by Tom McGregor
Illustrations on pages 22 and 23 supplied by Mary Evans Picture Library
Costume designs on page 69 by John Mollo
Grand Turk drawings on pages 60–1 by Tony Rimmington
The publishers would also like to thank Nicholas Blake for his assistance with this book

HarperCollins books may be purchased for educational, business, or sales promotional use.
For information please write: Special Markets Department,
HarperCollins Publishers Inc., 10 East 53rd Street, New York, NY 10022.

FIRST U.S. EDITION PUBLISHED 1999

ISBN 0-06-107357-1

10 9 8 7 6 5 4 3 2 1

Contents

Introduction

'Hornblower was at his station at the starboard quarterdeck carronades, his dirk at his side and a pistol in his belt . . . it was a moment for fast thinking ...'

C.S. Forester, Hornblower's creator, was a screenwriter as well as a novelist – and it shows. The above extract from *Mr. Midshipman Hornblower* cries out for a camera to film the exploits of fiction's most famous maritime hero.

Over the decades, countless attempts have been made by the television community to do just that. They all sank before they'd even set sail; scuttled by prose that tantalized the camera with one paragraph – and defeated it with the next:

'The tossing grey water of the Bay of Biscay was dotted with white sails as far as the eye could see, and although a strong breeze was blowing, every vessel was under perilously heavy canvas.'

And every television executive recoiled in horror, thwarted by the need for a perilously high budget, a sea uncluttered by tankers or windsurfers – and most of Nelson's Navy. The latter consideration has always been the main stumbling block in the crusade to bring *Hornblower* to the small screen. No realistic attempt could be made without building square-rigged sailing vessels, taking them out to sea, messing about with them, crippling some and sinking others. And no-one, until now, has successfully tackled and overcome that obstacle.

This is the story of how *Hornblower* made it from drawing board to drawing-room: of the genesis of one of the most ambitious, expensive, complex and challenging productions ever undertaken. It's about the making of ships, the mounting of expeditions, life on location, actors' attitudes and producers' problems. Cameras don't lie – they just tamper with the truth. And that truth is often stranger, funnier, more interesting, more surreal, more exciting and even more rewarding than the fiction that is *Hornblower*. This is the story, warts and all, from behind that camera . . .

The four two-hour films were developed by Celtic/Picture Palace Productions for Meridian Broadcasting in association with United Productions and A&E Network.

More than one hundred people have helped with this book. Producers and publicists, directors and drivers, editors and engineers, stuntmen and stars – every member of the cast and crew in the Ukraine, London and Portugal who has been pestered by the author has co-operated with unfailing enthusiasm and unflagging good humour.

Apologies that lack of space precludes the naming of names – but many thanks to them all.

CHAPTER ONE

Setting Sail

How it all began

It's midnight in mid-November. The Crimean mountains are wrapped up for winter in a layer of snow capped with an icy, clinging mist. The landscape is magisterial, eerily primeval; the silence profound.

But there is something moving on the mountain pass. It, too, is somewhat primeval: it is a nineteen-year-old Lada, spluttering and protesting as it struggles up the incline. Its shivering passenger, however, is not protesting. He is clutching a bottle of whisky with which he first made acquaintance fifteen hours earlier at Gatwick. Both he and the bottle are now somewhat exhausted, but the passenger – who has made this convoluted journey before – knows that it will end shortly at Yalta in a monolithic Soviet-built hotel with an (albeit temporary) lack of heating or hot water. For him, it's all part of the job – a job as a major television star who is filming one of the most ambitious TV dramas ever made.

Welcome (if the Lada makes it) to the set of *Hornblower*.

Two days later it's nine o'clock in the morning – and altogether a brighter story. The heating has been mended, the sun is beginning to shine and the Crimean mountains are (literally) behind the actor as he stands at the harbour waiting for a tug to take him half a mile out on the azure calm of the Black Sea. The actor has been up for nearly four hours in order to get into costume and make-up, but compared to some members of the crew, he's had something of a lie-in: he didn't have to be on set for the 6.30 a.m. call time.

The catering crew were up at 3.00 a.m.; likewise the second assistant director. Make-up and wardrobe were not far behind. Nineteen vehicles arrived at the Hotel Yalta to pick up the sound, special effects, stunts, first aid, electrical, camera and props departments, the producer and the director – all before dawn.

The Grand Turk *in full sail on the Black Sea. On one side, she is painted as an English ship for her starring role as the* Indefatigable. *On the other, she's dressed as a French ship to enable her to play supporting roles as enemy vessels.*

Seventy Ukrainian extras and twelve interpreters have joined the rest of the crew. Eight vessels of various descriptions complete the line-up. In total, there will be over two hundred cast and crew involved in this day's filming.

Approximately thirteen hours later the last scrap of make-up will have been removed, supper will have been served on set (the hotel's restaurants are closed for the winter) and the film unit will be back at base preparing for the morrow. If it has been a normal day's filming there will be roughly two minutes and ten seconds of air-time in the can.

Welcome to the set of one of the biggest, most challenging, most logistically complex and costliest productions ever undertaken in the history of British television.

With a romantic and resourceful hero, fictional stories set against factual backdrops, spectacular battle scenes and strong human elements of ambition, revenge, love, honour and betrayal, it's not surprising the Hornblower sagas have long been considered perfect vehicles for prime-time drama.

But, as with previous attempts to film them, this project looked like floundering and sinking because of the lack of another vehicle: a seaworthy square-rigged sailing ship of the 1790s. The few originals that survive – HMS *Trincomalee* at Hartlepool and the USS *Constitution* in Boston – are most definitely not for hire, and the cost of building one from scratch had television executives reeling in horror. More than two hundred years ago, Nelson's *Victory* cost £63,176 to build – a sum excluding the wages of two thousand shipwrights who worked on it at various times in the Chatham shipyards. And that was then . . .

Although a ship for *Hornblower* would be substantially smaller than Nelson's 100-gun ship-of-the-line, it would still be too costly and too time-consuming to commission.

Unless, by coincidence, it was already under construction . . .

In the Turkish port of Marmaris, a vessel was taking shape. It was originally to be called the *Phoenix*, an irony not lost on those who eventually saw it rise from the ashes of television's thwarted dreams.

The Grand Turk *under construction in the Marmaris shipyard.*

The keel takes shape. Every part of the Grand Turk, *internal and external, is designed and laid out on intricately detailed drawings (see page 60).*

THE BUILDING OF THE *GRAND TURK*

Michael Turk's family has an unbroken tradition of boat building, stretching back to the time of Richard the Lionheart. Early records document a Turk engaged in 1195 in the building of two galleys for 'Defense of the Realm' near the Tower of London. Since then, the Turks have made boats for English and foreign royalty as well as constructing fishing punts and passenger boats for the river Thames. Indeed the history of the Turks reflects a history of service to the Thames and Michael Turk, like many of his predecessors, has been a Swanmaster and Bargemaster to the Vintners' Company and is currently a Queen's Waterman. He is also a past Master of the Company of Watermen and Lightermen of the River Thames.

Yet from this splendidly arcane background, from roots firmly established in the past, springs a philosophy of constant development. For amongst their other activities the Turks have, since the 1930s, been involved in supplying ships of all sizes to film, television and commercial makers around the world. Their credits range from *A Man For All Seasons*, to James Bond and Indiana Jones films, to *Robin Hood, Prince of Thieves*, *Restoration* and, for television, *Minder*.

Which is why Michael Turk was in Marmaris with a pile of wood.

'We were originally building a twelfth-century merchant ship for a Schwarzenegger film that never got made,' says Mike Turk with a rueful smile. 'Then there was a film about Anne Bonney, the eighteenth-century female pirate – but that project collapsed as well.' Mike Turk is as unflappable as they come, but even he must have been irritated by the double blow. Much groundwork had already been done: the Iroko (a wood not unlike mahogany) had been imported to Turkey via France from Africa,

Mike Turk, owner and builder of the Grand Turk – *and Waterman to the Queen. His family has been building ships for 800 years – from passenger boats and fishing punts to pleasure craft for British and foreign royalty.*

selected in forty-foot logs in Istanbul and transported to Marmaris. There, in a ship-yard with a centuries-old tradition of building timber craft, part of it had already been cut to form a keel. And now no-one wanted the ship.

So Mike and his associates John Heath and Ian McDougal took matters into their own hands and built one anyway. 'It has always been my contention,' says Mike, 'that if there is a ship available, sea films will be made. But,' he admits, 'building this was a hell of a risk.'

It was a risk that paid off. At the same time as the associates decided on a square-rigged ship, the idea of filming Hornblower surfaced again. And for the first time in television history, the idea stayed afloat: in the shape of the *Grand Turk*, the first wooden British frigate to be built in over 140 years.

The statistics for the ship (see page 60) are truly impressive. And yet this seems a rather minimalist approach to film-making. After all, if you're intending to film major sea battles, surely you're going to need more than one ship?

Two years after that happy marriage in Marmaris and with filming under way, producer Andrew Benson grins at the question. 'Well,' he says, 'we're taking a lot of liberties . . . I hope the viewers think there are a lot of ships.'

Well, there aren't. Not that cameras lie – they just tamper with the truth. For in the making of *Hornblower*, only two sea-going square-rigged ships are being used: the *Grand Turk* and a Baltic trader called the *Julia*, built in the 1930s to a design that has changed little in over a hundred years. Apart from that, there is a great deal of artistic ingenuity – and eleven models. 'Not,' says Andrew Benson, 'your airfix-type models. These are upwards of five metres long and exact replicas of ships of the period.'

They are also – for such are the liberties taken in the film world – thousands of miles away in Petrozavodsk, north-west of St Petersburg, in a shipyard founded by Peter the Great of Russia. The finishing touches are being added and soon they will be en route to a tank in Pinewood Studios near London where they will play their part in the *Hornblower* saga.

But for the moment Andrew Benson is highlighting the other problems of bringing Forester's tales to the small screen. 'Most period drama,' he explains, 'is domestic and shot in England where we're lucky enough to have a wealth of historical locations – but here we're doing one at sea, so straight away you're talking abroad.'

Why?

The answer is obvious – when you think about it. The major criterion for filming *Hornblower* (after the ship problem) is the need for an uncluttered sea. Eighteenth-century midshipmen would fast lose their credibility if there was a windsurfer in the background or a jumbo jet flying overhead. The Black Sea coast off the Crimea has practically no traffic. Furthermore, the relatively unspoiled Crimean landscape also lends itself to the first two episodes. For while the greater part of those episodes is shot at sea, the land-based scenes require only small sets, easily borrowed or built and dis-mantled, and spaces uncluttered by telegraph poles. Thus the Lamb Inn at Spithead is

OPPOSITE *The Baltic trader* Julia *against the backdrop of the Crimean mountains. Built in the 1930s to a design that hasn't changed for hundreds of years, it is the only other full-sized ship used in the making of* Hornblower.

OPPOSITE AND BELOW
The models are miniature replicas of full-scale ships of the period and are seaworthy with fully-functional rigging. As none of the ships were designed to be seen from close-up, some of the deck detail has been simplified. The only twentieth-century intrusion comes with the cannons: without twelve-inch sailors to fire them, they are operated by remote control. Built of pine and birch, each ship took an average of five men five weeks to construct. The largest – that of the thirty-foot 74-gun Justinian – took three months to build.

actually half an inn near Artek harbour, while the Admiralty headquarters in Gibraltar is, in fact, the Livadia Palace in Yalta – the location of the Yalta Conference at the end of the Second World War.

Nevertheless, filming in the Crimea has its disadvantages. 'The infrastructure,' explains Andrew Benson, 'is very poor. And the cultural and language difficulties are enormous. The Ukraine, quite frankly, isn't equipped with all the things we take for granted in Western Europe in terms of film support. So we had to take everything we might possibly need – including the proverbial kitchen sink.'

So, having resolved the problems of finding a square-rigged ship and a suitable location, the entire production team headed for the Ukraine. Eleven articulated lorries hurtled through Europe carrying everything from cameras to wind machines, wigs to woofers, breeches to baked beans. About the only thing they weren't allowed to bring was gunpowder; that had to be ordered from Kiev. But Andrew Benson wasn't exaggerating: the cultural and language differences are enormous. They were sent 270 kilos of napalm instead. 'Bizarre,' says one incredulous member of the crew. 'We sent it back.'

CHAPTER TWO

The Battle of the Black Sea

Filming in the Crimea

The actor is now being transported to the *Grand Turk*. In place of a cramped, uncomfortable Lada is a cramped, uncomfortable inflatable dinghy crashing over the choppy surface of the Black Sea. It will take forty minutes to reach the *Grand Turk* and by that time everyone in the dinghy – the marine engineer, the actor, the make-up artist and the second assistant director – will have a sore bottom: unless, like Jordi Casares, you are standing up. It seems an impossible feat of balance. He must be showing off. After all, Jordi is an ex-stuntsman and now stunt co-ordinator on *Hornblower*. As a veteran of Indiana Jones and James Bond movies, of the *Sharpe* television series and that other film about boats, *Titanic*, standing upright in an unstable craft going at speed ought to be as easy as falling off a log to Jordi. No, he says with a rueful grin; he is not showing off. 'People may *think* I'm showing off – but it's quite the opposite. I've got two pins in my hip and it hurts to sit down in this.'

Just another example of all not being quite as it seems.

The *Grand Turk*, too, is not quite the ship it appears – as anyone being helped aboard with the occupants of the inflatable would soon realize. For while there are plenty of people milling about looking as if they had just stepped out of Nelson's navy, there are also two distinctly modern and distinctly separate crews. One is the film crew: the other the ship's crew. The *Grand Turk* may be a stage set, but it's also a sea-going vessel and, like any other, needs a captain and crew to operate it.

That captain is Clive 'Topsy' Toner – and he looks the part. Tall and imposing, he could well be an actor who grew his luxuriant beard especially for his role in

Hornblower shows his mettle as he boards the Marie Galante.

ABOVE *Topsy Toner,
captain of the* Grand Turk.

Hornblower. But no. He is actually a bona fide sailor, with twenty-five years in the navy behind him as well as several years crewing and then captaining a square-rigged training ship in the Caribbean. As for a new career as a movie star, he'll have to rethink the beard. 'I can't be in the film *because* of my beard,' he explains (with a faint hint of regret). 'Apparently a few sailors did have beards in those days, but they weren't supposed to. The ship's barber shaved them once a week – and I'm certainly not shaving mine.'

So no film career for Topsy – and anyway he has enough to do behind the scenes. It is he who took the boat from Marmaris to Yalta; he who, with the crew of twelve, fitted the running rigging; and it is Topsy who steers the ship out to sea every morning and back into the narrow harbour every evening.

It's that last task that preys on Topsy's mind every day. The harbour, while well protected, is also small – and the *Grand Turk*, although easily manoeuvrable with its two engines and bow-thruster, is both extremely high-sided and extremely tall. 'You've got a lot of windage up there,' explains Topsy as he looks up at the 120-foot main mast, 'and the ship doesn't draw very much: there's nothing under the water in comparison to the height of the rig. I can't afford to crunch the ship,' he finishes, ''cause if I do that we've got no film.'

Topsy's words serve as a reminder that, while cultural and language difficulties are usually resolvable, watery ones are not. If you're filming at sea you are at the mercy of that

RIGHT *'Actors,' says Robert Bathurst (Lieutenant Eccleston), 'are like the ropes on a ship. There's loads of them hanging around apparently doing nothing – but they're all supposed to have a purpose.' Here he is (centre) being purposeful with cast and crew on the poop deck.*

Swinging from the rigging. The 'topmen' – sailors who work aloft – are, in Hornblower, *Ukrainian naval cadets. The little people in the red coats below are actors.*

sea: and the Black Sea is no exception. Being inland, it isn't tidal, but the winds sweeping in from the south and the mountains on its north coast contribute to its notorious swell. 'Ships get pounded to pieces here,' interjects Mike Turk with a cheerful grin . 'The winds can come up in an instant – and we've had some real thumpers.' But not as bad as the thumpers in 1992: in that year a ship was blown straight over the harbour wall.

Apart from ensuring that the *Grand Turk* doesn't suffer the same fate, Topsy is also in an anomalous position as regards the film crew: he is not one of their number, yet their instructions have to be relayed through him to the 'real' crew. Set dresser Jan Chaney explains that if sails are to be unfurled for a certain scene, then she will ask Topsy, who will in turn instruct his crew – who will then supervise the Ukrainian naval cadets (film extras who act as 'topmen') as they are filmed climbing the rigging and unfurling the sails. 'It *is* unusual,' says Jan. 'But then film sets don't normally have a captain.'

And ships don't normally have a film set on board.

Yet the two disciplines, seemingly poles apart, are remarkably similar in their hierarchical structures – part of the reason, no doubt, why the two crews work so well together. Where Topsy is in charge of the ship's crew, Andrew Grieve, the director of *Hornblower*, is in charge of the film crew. And where the chief officer is Topsy's deputy, so the first assistant director is Andrew Grieve's – and so on.

In a rare and brief moment of relaxation between takes, Andrew Grieve sits on a cannon and surveys the deck of the *Grand Turk*. There isn't, in truth, much of the deck to see – it's almost completely covered with actors, crew, cameras, wind machines and

The aftermath of a battle at sea. Make-up artist Veyatie Macleod bays for more blood. It's when shooting this sort of scene that the cramped conditions on board the Grand Turk *become most apparent. In Nelson's time, the sides of the decks (and the surgeon's cockpit) were often painted red to make the blood of the dead and wounded 'blend in' with the surroundings . . .*

assorted paraphernalia that would have had Nelson turning in his grave. Andrew Grieve is hinting – not very convincingly – that he too will soon be in his grave. 'It's the most difficult set I've ever had to contend with,' he muses. 'It's the only one that moves both up and down and from side to side. It's got too many people on it – some of whom are seasick. And it's slow work because of the difficulties of finding people, moving them around and positioning the ship.'

So why on earth does he do it?

'Aversion therapy. I've been trying to give it up for forty years.'

A blatant lie.

But he's not lying about the challenges of filming on board – and in particular the problems of manoeuvring the ship. For Topsy's role is far from over when the ship is out at sea: he has a constant battle to reconcile the elements with the requirements of filming. And it is Andrew Grieve who gives the orders for the battle.

The main criterion for the vast majority of filming at sea is not to show the land. Given that they are pretending to be far from shore in the Bay of Biscay but are, in fact,

It's very important for the camera department to know the length of the actors' noses.

21

Propmaster Brian Henry winning the cannon-carrying contest. This cannon is, in fact, made from fibreglass to enable the crew to move it around and bury people under it without killing them (see page 20). All the other cannons on board, however, are made from cast iron.

less than a mile from the mountainous Crimean coast, this is understandable. What is not so easy to grasp is the fact that they can't overcome this by placing the cameraman with his back to the land and just getting on with it. Each shot has to have a 'reverse' (think of a conversation between two characters standing opposite each other: the camera has to show both points of view). That is standard in film-making – but not so easily achieved when the considerations of sun, wind, land and the swell of the sea are thrown in.

'It's like playing some terrible kind of three-dimensional chess in your head,' says Andrew Grieve. 'If we have the sails up the ship's much steadier – but then it will sway in an arc of 180 degrees and the wind is usually blowing in such a way (from the south) that it will arc towards the land. Dealing with the wind, tide, sun, the angle you want to shoot at and taking into account the reverses at the same time is . . . well,' he finishes with a smile of resignation, 'you have very little control.'

Unusually for a director, Andrew Grieve is used to messing about in boats. Before embarking on a career in film he spent four years in the merchant navy. 'I still sail a lot,' he adds, 'and I've mugged up on my terminology for this ship. I know pretty much what everything is and what it can do. It does help!'

And then, as if to illustrate his point about having little control over the elements, the *Grand Turk* pitches and rolls in the sudden swell. The movement is surprising rather than violent, yet there are crashing sounds from below decks and a spot of drunken lurching on deck. Above, the Ukrainian naval cadet on the main mast's fighting top finds himself above the sea rather than the deck: he has swung thirty feet to the left. Andrew Grieve instinctively braces himself against the cannon. The person sitting beside him, who has yet to develop sea legs, falls off and lands in a little heap beside the gun carriage. No-one else seems remotely perturbed by the pitching. They have long since learned to walk with slightly splayed feet; they have recovered from the effects of their first days on board (falling over in the shower back at base is the most common), and a sudden swell is, after all, a small matter compared to the storms that can hurl ships over harbour walls.

But Andrew Grieve won the terrible game of three-dimensional chess he played in his head: time and tide notwithstanding, he never lost a day's filming at sea.

BELOW DECKS

The companionways and ladders leading down to the upper and lower decks of the *Grand Turk* may only span a few feet – but they also leap across two centuries. All is modernity below decks. There is a kitchen, there are showers and lavatories and six twin cabins with all mod cons. This may sound rather promising for the actors: a reward for their experiences in Ladas, Soviet-style hotels and cramped inflatables. It isn't. Kitchen apart, the modern facilities are out-of-bounds for the cast and film crew: they are the living quarters for Topsy's men. The cast and crew of *Hornblower* have to make do with the wardroom, which is oddly spartan, not to say makeshift.

This is because the *Grand Turk* is still in the process of being built. Its exterior is complete, but the interior, in estate agent's parlance, merely 'has potential'. And that potential will be fulfilled when the *Grand Turk* sails into its next incarnation – as an exhibit and venue for corporate entertainment during the Millennium celebrations. For the moment, it is basic, cramped and crowded. There is nowhere – above or below decks – for anyone to go to seek privacy during the twelve-hour days on board. It's a far cry from the land of the Hollywood trailer – and nobody minds. Again and again, cast and crew alike repeat that the *Hornblower* production is one of the happiest ships (pun intended) they have worked on; that being thrown together in such close proximity for so long has resulted in an extraordinary camaraderie both on and off set.

The upper deck on the Grand Turk. *This is as luxurious as it gets during the twelve hours spent at sea each day. There would have been substantially less headroom in a real frigate of the era. The* Grand Turk's *designers 'missed out' a deck to create more space (there is one deck below this: historically there would have been two).*

There is ample evidence of that below decks. A famous actor is playing chess with the catering assistant; the *Grand Turk*'s electrical engineer (who occasionally dons a wet-suit to jump overboard to retrieve a lost cutlass) is chatting to another actor; other members of the ship's company are drinking coffee, laughing together, reading or snatching forty winks with their heads in their hands on a trestle table.

The camera, however, is a different matter: it never ventures below and all the interior scenes are shot elsewhere. Far from being a case of gratuitous liberty-taking, this is a necessity. For had the *Grand Turk* been accurate in every detail, it would have had considerably less headroom: barely five feet, in the case of the lower deck. Not exactly suitable for modern purposes. As Mike Turk explains, 'We missed out a deck below. We've only got a lower deck with accommodation, engines and hydraulics and then a through deck with galley and the wardroom.'

The pontoon, with the Grand Turk *in the background. Most scenes showing ships' interiors were shot here. The structure was a scale model of a quarter of a 74-gun ship-of-the-line and could be towed out to sea. It was dismantled and destroyed after filming in the Crimea.*

The solution to the problem of filming the interiors lies in one of the strangest structures ever to grace the waters of the Black Sea. Back in Artek harbour, there sits a flat-bottomed barge with what looks like quarter of a ship sitting on top of it. On closer inspection, it turns out to be exactly that: a slice of a 74-gun ship-of-the-line sitting atop a pontoon. Open to the elements on three sides, it has several levels, companionways and rooms. While some walls give on to open sea and ladders lead nowhere, the set has everything required for filming the interior scenes – including low deckheads.

Andrew Grieve is full of praise for this unlikely-looking construction. 'It gives a tremendous sense of place. You can hear the water slapping against it so you feel you're on a real ship. And the deckheads are so low you can see them in almost every shot. On a normal set you never see the ceiling.' Other members of the crew were less enthusiastic: they kept walloping their heads against the ceilings.

But the pontoon provided more than just interiors: the structure also doubled as the deck of the *Justinian*, Hornblower's first ship and the vessel featured in the first two acts of episode one, 'The Even Chance'. For while artistic ingenuity enabled the *Grand Turk* to 'play' the *Indefatigable* and three other frigates (with the result that it was actually firing on itself) it could not masquerade as a much larger ship-of-the-line. A little more ingenuity – and the peculiar pontoon – did the trick. Later in the episode, when the *Justinian* is seen from a distance, the reality is even stranger: the ship is one of the thirty-foot models and the sequence, along with every other scene involving more than two ships, was filmed three months later in the tank at Pinewood Studios.

But, for the moment, we're still in the Black Sea . . .

LEFT *Peter 'Wingnut' Wallace, the* Grand Turk's *electrical engineer with the cutlass he's just retrieved from the sea. It's made from rubber: while the actors had real (although disabled) weapons, they also had rubber ones for close combat fighting.*

CENTRE *Robert Lindsay and Ioan Gruffudd pretending they're in a Hollywood trailer. This, the sound department's rickety van, is as close as they'll get.*

RIGHT *Stunt co-ordinator Jordi Casares.*

CHAPTER THREE

Landing in Portugal

Filming on the Iberian Peninsula

Had *Hornblower* stayed any later in the Crimea, the production would have suffered the same fate as Napoleon himself: defeat at the hands of the Russian winter. As it was, they cut things fine by leaving in mid-December. The diesel in the pantechnicons froze solid in Kiev, icicles formed in the production office, and the Hotel Yalta closed.

This last event came as something of a shock to Richard Whitehead who was finalizing the removal of *Hornblower's* freight – he was still staying there. In a scenario reminiscent of Jack Nicholson's performance in *The Shining*, he was left rattling around a hotel the size of a planet with no heating, barely any electricity and no food. Jack Nicholson went mad and took up axe-wielding. Richard Whitehead was on his own for a week with a telephone, a heater and a light bulb and is, by all accounts, still sane.

After Yalta, the production continued apace in London. There may have been a five-month 'break' before filming in Portugal, but there wasn't so much as a pause for the production team. The footage in the can went into post-production; the Portugal shoot into pre-production. So while the filmed material was being edited, while music was composed and effects were being added, the next scripts were being finalized; recces were undertaken in Portugal; design, costume and crew prepared for the next shoot; and accommodation, drivers and a Portuguese crew were located and booked. Innumerable other tasks had to be completed to set up the whole circus again before the wagons could roll into Portugal – including the preparation and six weeks of filming

The set at Muzillac in 'The Frogs and the Lobsters' episode. Half the buildings have been standing for two hundred years – the other half for two weeks. 'It's a great compliment,' says production designer Rob Harris, 'when people think we've spent weeks building absolutely nothing.' (Everything on the right of the picture is new.)

of the models. Finally, in May, the unit reassembled in the town of Sesimbra, forty kilometres south of Lisbon.

The contrast between this old fishing village with its Moorish castle on the cliff and Yalta (twinned with Margate) is astonishing. And the journey from London – a two-hour flight followed by a forty-minute drive that takes you across the (newly opened) longest bridge in Europe – is a far cry from the convoluted journey to the Crimea. And Lisbon is a capital city everyone wants to see. No-one wanted to visit poor old Simferopol (rhymes with, and now known as, Simplyawful), the Crimean capital.

It doesn't take much prompting, however, for people to remember that being in Yalta was – inconveniences aside – a fascinating and rare experience. 'I was tremendously excited by it,' says actor Robert Bathurst. 'Russia's recent history is extraordinary and so was the Crimea. And if the people didn't smile much at first . . . well, can you blame them? They don't exactly have a lot to smile about.' Others agree, and add that if you look beneath the surface you'll find plenty of smiles. 'The image that's painted of dark, grey people isn't really true,' says Ioan Gruffudd. 'Someone on a Russian production invited me to his birthday party. It started at midday and went on to nine. It was fantastic – they were extraordinarily generous. We really entered the Chekhovian spirit . . .'

But there's no doubt that life is easier in sunny Sesimbra, on a personal as well as a professional level. The seafood is wonderful and plentiful, restaurants proliferate and the accommodation is quite the opposite of simply awful. It would be a great place for a holiday – but film crews don't appear to have holidays. Andrew Benson will have worked solidly for twenty months. His assistant Dani Gordon, in contrast, leads a charmed life: she had a week off last year. Adele Steward, the production co-ordinator, sits at a desk for at least fourteen hours a day and, like many other 'behind-the-scenes' people, never even sees the film sets. Or the sun.

But the crew of the *Grand Turk* and the *Julia* have been at sea for five weeks. After leaving Yalta, the *Grand Turk* returned to Marmaris where more work on the interior was carried out. The master's and owner's cabins were built and, to the huge relief of the entire film crew, the portaloos in the forecastle were replaced with real ones. In April she set sail for Sesimbra, via Rhodes, the Corinth Canal, Sicily, the Balearic Islands, Spain and Gibraltar. Ian McDougal, the ship's master, recalls that the *Grand Turk* caused some consternation in the Corinth Canal: they're not used to frigates of Nelson's era, bristling with cannons. 'It took some time to persuade them that the cannons weren't real.'

Outside the canal they were enveloped in serious fog. As they had no radar at the time, the situation could have been serious: sixty containers lost from a Greek cargo vessel in a storm were floating, half-submerged, on the same transit line as the *Grand Turk*. Had they collided, the ship would have been holed and *Hornblower* would have sunk to a watery grave.

But they arrived in Sesimbra without mishap – although they were two weeks late. Ian McDougal recounts that they were delayed by travelling westwards into a westerly wind (a problem familiar to Hornblower) and by violent storms. Listening to the crew talk about the conditions they encountered in the Atlantic, it's clear that they didn't have a lot of fun on the last stretch: at one point the entire bowsprit of the *Grand Turk* was under water. At other times, with the wind against them, they were only able to reach a speed of one knot.

Yet they arrived in Portugal just in time for filming to begin on schedule. Andrew Benson recalls how relieved he was that the *Grand Turk*, the entire cast and crew and all the various back-up units were established in the same place, at the same time – and in western Europe. 'I looked out of my window on the day before filming began, saw the familiar landscape, blue skies, calm sea and a happy crew lying by the pool. It was fantastic. And even though the boat was late, we still managed to get her ready in time and – something that wasn't needed on the Black Sea – to obtain our MSA (Marine Safety Association) certificate.' This involved a man flying out from England to inspect the boat and to declare her seaworthy and safe. He issued the certificate on Saturday, just two days before filming was to begin.

And then, on Monday, disaster struck. 'Whatever I do, however much I prepare,' sighs Andrew Benson, 'I am not King Canute.' That's probably just as well – look what happened to him. But the point is clear: no producer in the world can govern the seas, and especially not the Atlantic when it decides to stage a full-scale storm, without warning, on the day *Hornblower* was going to set sail. The azure skies and calm sea disappeared – and with them the film crew's plans.

With the *Grand Turk* rolling about in the harbour, there was no way they could film on board – but there was a way they could film. All along, the shooting schedule had built in 'weather cover' to cater for such an eventuality: other, interior scenes were earmarked to take the place of the scenes at sea. So it was that the crew moved inland to film in the captain's cabin. 'Like us and many of the other props,' says Andrew Benson, 'it had been ferried from Yalta to the UK, refurbished and then taken to Portugal.' Production designer Rob Harris and his team then re-erected it in a warehouse and the unit moved in to film while the storm raged at sea.

Two days later, conditions had improved enough to enable them to board the *Grand Turk*; and that was as far as many of them got. Forty-eight people were seasick within the first two hours – a far higher tally than the Black Sea ever managed to claim. Sod's Law was being implemented with a vengeance: a bitter irony against those who thought that filming in Portugal would be 'easier'.

Director Andrew Grieve says that filming on the Atlantic was actually far more difficult than on the Black Sea. 'We got used to the prevailing conditions off Yalta. Here we were bouncing around a lot more – and the wind was more difficult to deal with.' He skips neatly over the seasickness scenario (as would any self-respecting sea-faring

director if he were one of the victims himself . . .) But 'Making of' books ought to tell the whole truth – including the fact that the *Grand Turk* had to be hosed down that evening, inside and out, by the Sesimbra fire service. A very un-Hornblower-like little drama.

Apart from the seasickness – and the presence of distinctly twentieth-century speed-boats, jet-skis and fishing boats – all has gone according to plan. At Sesimbra there are none of the basic logistical problems described in Andrew Benson's words: 'Oh my God the actors are coming off set and there's nothing for them to eat, they're wet, there's no hot water and no electricity.' Nor are there any problems with the phones, the roads, the faxes, fuel, safety vessels or rats. Everyone's happy.

Laura Anne Sprawson, ten-year-old daughter of the unit carpenter, is ecstatic. She's been given a part as an extra. At the beginning of 'The Duchess and the Devil', Hornblower and his division capture the French sloop *Le Reve*, hurling a French look-out boy into the Atlantic in the process. It would have been quite easy to lure a child off the beach and then throw it overboard, but this was deemed a little rash. Laura Anne, visiting her father on location, was both ready and willing – and a strong swimmer. Even so, and invisible on screen, there's a rowing boat only three feet away as she lands – and a diver right beside her.

Hornblower and Moncoutant (Antony Sher) – and signs of future dissent. This interior of Pellew's cabin was actually a land-based set.

Part of the reason for choosing Sesimbra was that beyond the headland there is a vast area of protected national park. It's green, unspoiled by tourism, unsullied by modern buildings, and probably looks exactly as it did in the eighteenth century. Both scripts require land in the background, so there is no visual trickery needed to provide it.

The only coastal shot on which they cheated was of the Spanish fort in 'The Duchess and the Devil'. It looks as if it's sitting right above the sea. It's not. The Castle of Sesimbra has been sitting on its hill behind the town for well over a thousand years. The *Hornblower* camera crew moved it by, in layman's terms, shooting an empty cliff beside the sea, then the fort, and sticking the two together.

Now, at the end of the first week in June and after three weeks on the Atlantic, filming at sea is finished and the *Grand Turk*, the *Julia* and *Hornblower* part company, all moving on to further adventures. The *Grand Turk* is earmarked to play a prominent part in the Millennium celebrations, and Hornblower's going to make fireworks as well, for the recces that were done earlier in the year were largely about finding suitable places to blow up.

The first set used after leaving the *Grand Turk* is Quinta da Conceicao, a large and extremely beautiful country house with extensive grounds and fine architectural details of Hornblower's period. It is currently for sale for several million pounds although prospective buyers may be put off by the fact that part of the British Navy, a French émigré army, the 95th Light Infantry and a clutch of peasants have moved in, turned it into the town of Muzillac, and are in the process of recreating the Revolutionary Wars.

There's also a guillotine in the back garden.

Rob Harris is the man who paved the way for this campaign. The production designer on *Hornblower*, he's responsible for creating all the sets to be used in these episodes. 'This,' he says as he looks at what he has done, 'was the first major build, so it took slightly longer than we'd hoped. It's always the same with the first one in a foreign country; you have to assess how that country works.'

Not very well, by the looks of things. They spent five weeks here and they don't seem to have done anything except wheel the guillotine in and chop down the telephone wires.

Rob is used to remarks like that. 'It's a great compliment when people ask why it's taken so long to do nothing. The point is that it takes a long time to *look* as if you've done nothing.'

What Rob has done is really quite spectacular. He's added extensively to the eighteenth-century outbuildings of Quinta da Conceicao so that it's impossible for the naked eye to discern what is and isn't authentic. And he's done it in such a way that the camera can film from all angles and turn the place into a town.

There are seven structures, including an inn, several houses and even a pigsty, that are brand new. And then there are the details added to existing buildings. The Marquis

Moncoutant took this guillotine from England to use on the French who had turned Republican. The film crew used it to chop melons. It's a perfect – and lethal – replica of Dr Guillotine's invention.

The crest on Moncoutant's house (see previous page). The house itself is over two hundred years old, but the glue has barely dried on the crest. It's a Hornblower addition and is made of polystyrene.

de Moncoutant's house – the real manor house – now sports the nobleman's crest on the side facing the 'town square'. It looks both authentic and substantial, but it's neither. It's made from polystyrene.

Everything, in fact, looks far more substantial than it is (except, one hopes, the original buildings), but nothing is so flimsy that it will collapse like a pack of cards. Rob explains, 'The sets have to be strong enough to withstand high winds, but the recent spell of wet weather was problematic. The walls are basically plaster applied to chipboard, so when moisture seeps in and then dries out, the plaster cracks.'

There are, of course, lots of cracks in the buildings anyway – but you can't have them changing daily. Fortunately for *Hornblower*, the existing buildings haven't been particularly well maintained and look as if they could well have served in the French Revolution. Paradoxically, it takes quite a lot of maintenance to keep the new additions looking scruffy. 'We spend half an hour every morning touching them up,' explains Rob.

The trouble is, so do lots of other people. When buildings look so real, the temptation is to treat them as such, to lean against them and poke them with swords. The Portuguese extra lolling against a door-frame is doing just that. Dressed as an émigré soldier, battle-scarred and weary in the intense heat, he looks the picture of authenticity. Then he stops fiddling with his sword as the director calls 'action'. A brief silence descends as the camera rolls. Then Hornblower strides into view and makes for the schoolhouse (one of the original outbuildings) where he will find Mariette. He calls out her name: another silence descends.

It's broken, not by a tentative 'Horatio?' from Mariette but by the sound of the twentieth century echoing through Muzillac. Someone's mobile phone has started to ring.

The director's reaction is unprintable.

The Muzillac shoot lasts for eight days, and, apart from the production office which will remain at the hotel in Sesimbra, the entire unit moves here for that period. A few hundred yards from the set, a tent the size of a ballroom is erected for the wardrobe department (they have to cater for several hundred extras), two huge lunch tents are pitched nearby and, scattered around, various generators, support vehicles, dozens of cars, and, in a real departure from anything seen in the Crimea, the Winnebagos (trailers) for the principal actors.

Andrew Grieve is characteristically blunt about the Winnebagos, dismissing the notion that they are divisive and introduce an 'us and them' element into this egalitarian production. 'I don't give a stuff if any of the actors as *people* are tired, I care about whether they are tired as actors. That shows on screen. Those with most to do need peace and quiet to learn their lines and as much rest as possible – particularly in this heat (it's nearly 90 degrees). I don't want them to be sweat-soaked and grumpy. If they didn't need the Winnies they wouldn't get them. But there's no question of them getting above themselves.'

It sums up the relationships on set. Winnebagos notwithstanding, this is still the non-hierarchical production of the Crimean days. There is no rank-pulling; there are no chairs with 'Director' splayed across the back, and at lunchtime everyone stands in

Hornblower in trouble in Muzillac as the Republican troops advance. For close-up action sequences, a riot shield is placed in front of the camera.

OVERLEAF *Republican troops overwhelm Muzillac, and Hornblower (centre) battles his way to rescue Mariette. The Republican troops' legionnaire-type helmets were as much about fashion as function. With the Roman excavations at Herculaneum, the French were heavily influenced by classicism. Other influences – like the fur on their helmets – crept in from the Hungarian and Croatian borders of Europe.*

the same queue. In the long line that is already snaking out from the catering van, Cherie Lunghi, resplendent as the Duchess of Wharfedale, is chatting to the Portuguese chippie, Antony Sher is deep in conversation with Paul the focus-puller and poor old Ioan Gruffudd is being pestered by the author who has constantly been haranguing him for a chat over lunch.

It's a far cry from productions, both in Hollywood and Britain, where 'stars' talk only to God, take a tape measure to their Winnies – and refuse to work if they're too short.

Back on set an hour later and people from the props department are slicing melons with the guillotine while Charmian the set dresser pours blood on the ground in front of it. Make-up chief Veyatie Macleod is checking that the afternoon's activities – including the decapitation of Antony Sher – will, months in the future, be transmitted after the nine o'clock watershed. 'It's going to be rather gory,' she says, 'and can't be shown before then.'

'Gory?' Andrew Grieve is scathing. 'There's only two pints of blood. They used to execute six hundred people a day in Paris. Imagine how much blood there was then.'

Method acting. The concept of Liberty, Egality and Fraternity applies to the dead as well as the living. The schedule has to cater for the fact that the goriest scenes must be transmitted after the nine o'clock watershed. This, however, will remain firmly behind the scenes.

They also used to have *tricoteuses* gathered round the guillotine as it scythed its way through the population of Paris. In an uncanny echo of that grim spectacle, one of the actors (it probably wouldn't do his reputation a great deal of good to divulge his name) is doing his embroidery as he watches the melon-slicing.

At the other end of the town of Muzillac – i.e. a hundred yards away – Gerry the medic is taking several people's blood pressure. 'Some of them do actually have high blood pressure and have to be careful in the heat. But it's funny,' he adds. 'Every time I take out my bag to minister to someone, lots of people come running. There's a sort of "me too please" mentality about medicine.'

Gerry finishes taking blood pressure and begins to slap some sun-tan lotion on. Derek from special effects sees him and comes trotting over. 'Me too, please, Gerry.' Several other people follow him.

But Antony Sher doesn't need any sun-tan cream. His face is liberally covered in blood from being mauled by the Muzillac mob (alias Veyatie) and, in an hour or so, he will be lying face-up on the guillotine, about to breathe his last as the Marquis de Moncoutant.

The unit abandons Muzillac that evening and shooting begins next morning at a new location. It's the Palace of Calhariz, and it makes the previous location look positively tawdry by comparison. The vast seventeenth-century mansion is one of the homes of the Marquis of Palmela, whose family still own vast swathes of the Arrabida region. The palace is now used as a holiday home and, having undergone extensive renovation on the exterior and the outbuildings, the interior is now being touched up. The Duke, looking every inch the Portuguese aristocrat with his Lobb shoes and Turnbull & Asser shirt, is wandering around, unobtrusively keeping an eye on his heirlooms. For the place is bursting with antiques, and he's given the crew free rein to use many of them, including the family silver which has just been polished in a kitchen the size of an aircraft hangar. But he's hidden the visitors' book lest someone write 'Hornblower was here' under the names of two distinguished house guests: Queen Elizabeth and Prince Philip.

Yesterday the crew was filming part of episode four: today it's back to episode three, *The Duchess and the Devil*. Two rooms of the Palace of Calhariz are being used as interiors of the 'fort' commandant's quarters: the grand hall as the dining room and an anteroom as the Duchess's bedroom. The lights and camera have been set up in the former to film the dinner party scene where a French artillery officer 'outs' the Duchess as the actress Katherine Cobham. The Duchess, of course, *is* an actress: Cherie Lunghi. She comes flying back from lunch, takes one look at the camera, says 'Oh God, it's pointing at me,' and then takes her seat opposite it. Then she looks down at her plate and laughs. Brian Henry from props has painted stupid faces on everyone's quail's eggs. Now he's rushing about with a plastic bag filled with garnish. Continuity is all: this morning's parsley has wilted and needs to be replaced.

RIGHT *Don Massaredo (Ronald Pickup) and Hornblower in the dining room of the Palace of Calhariz (Don Massaredo's quarters within the Spanish fort).*

OPPOSITE *The 'Duchess of Wharfedale' (Cherie Lunghi) isn't above flirting with the infatuated Hornblower on the terrace. The blue and white 'azulejos' tiles are distinctively Portuguese – and now extremely valuable. It's no longer possible to reproduce the blue that, here, dates from the seventeenth century.*

Outside, in the palace's riding stables, stunt co-ordinator Jordi Casares is teaching a French general how to ride, some English pressmen have arrived and are beginning to wish they hadn't as the temperature soars to 100 degrees. Andrew Benson, meanwhile, is telling them why Portugal is such a perfect place to film. 'The location for these episodes had to meet two main criteria: a sheltered harbour with a relatively quiet sea and nearby land-based locations that could double as both France and Spain. Also, we needed old castles on hills and, vitally, somewhere without skyscrapers and pylons all over the place.'

The protected area of the Arrabida fitted the bill on all counts, and an added bonus was the extraordinarily arid land. No lush vegetation can grow here; the landscape hasn't changed for hundreds of years and the massive poppies wafting in the wind are the same as those that grow in similarly poor soil in France and Spain.

Several miles away, however, some of the poppies have been trampled underfoot in the course of a massive building operation that, after the better part of seven weeks, has just been completed. This, the most complex land-based build on the entire shoot, is the bridge at Muzillac – fifteen minutes' transmission time but an hour's drive from the Muzillac set itself. It's also the most ambitious project undertaken by the set designer.

The bridge has to be strong enough to withstand the weight of a hundred and fifty horses and men, impressive enough to play an important part in 'The Frogs and The Lobsters' story and realistic enough to look as if it's been in situ for well over two hundred years.

So why didn't they just use a real bridge?

'Because,' says Rob Harris, 'we have to blow it up, and you can't go around blowing up other people's ancient structures for the sake of a few minutes of film.'

You can, however, build an entirely new, 45-metre-long bridge out of scaffolding and plywood, cover it with polystyrene 'stone' and then paint and dress it to look . . . to look as if the art department have done absolutely nothing at all. The bridge at Muzillac is, to all intents and purposes, a real bridge. And after a week's filming it will be an ex-bridge. Several of the crew are slightly apprehensive about filming its destruction – a vital part of the story. Andrew Grieve is refreshingly brusque about it. 'We'll only get one chance at it, so we'll position as many cameras as we can afford and then blow the bugger up.' In fact, when the time came to blow up the bridge on camera, the combination of a well-constructed bridge and an underestimated explosive charge meant that little happened and it had to be blown up a second time.

The bridge, by coincidence, is on an estate whose owners also have a television studio on their land, so they're used to film crews and their antics.

Other people are not. The *Hornblower* crew and their props have aroused great curiosity in Sesimbra and its environs. One holidaying couple asked what the *Grand Turk* was doing floating about at sea. When told it was being used to make a film, they replied, 'Oh. We thought it was a ship.'

A week later, day-trippers going from Setubal to Troia were slightly alarmed by their fellow passengers on the ferry: the entire 95th Light Infantry, a French Republican

Building bridges. The most ambitious set-build nears completion.

army and – even more bizarrely dressed – a film crew. For Troia was the setting for another of the most ambitious of Hornblower's exploits: the landing on the beach at Muzillac. In terms of numbers, it was *the* most ambitious: the cast, crew and 250 extras landed on the beach in an operation that lasted three days and was fraught with potential hazards. In the event, in the words of Andrew Grieve, 'it went extremely well'.

But, echoing Andrew Benson's words after the storm that scuppered filming at sea, there is no guarantee that anything is ever going to go – either well or at all. 'You can make any number of contingency plans,' he says. 'You prepare and plan down to the last detail; you think you've catered for every eventuality – but the reality of the filming process is that there are still a million and one things that can go wrong at the last moment.'

The bridge doesn't just have to look real – it has to bear the weight of hundreds of horses and men. It also has to be blown up with as much care as it was built: you can't have bits of scaffolding flying about in the eighteenth century . . .

Another reality is that you shouldn't tempt fate by uttering words like that. Andrew Benson wasn't to learn of the events until later that evening, but as he was speaking Estelle Skornik fell and twisted her ankle, a horse reversed into the first assistant director's car and shattered the windscreen and, just for good measure, a rather famous actor due on set the next day was phoning from London to say that he was terribly sorry but his passport was out of date and was there anything Andrew could do about it?

Two hours later there was a power cut and half the text of this book vanished into the ether. There wasn't anything anyone could do – apart from phone Andrew Benson to say, 'I'm terribly sorry, but is there anything you can do about it?'

For the producer of *Hornblower*, whether he likes it or not, is all things to all people on set. He might be making the most complex drama ever shown on British television, but he's also required to be a doctor, mechanic, diplomat and magician.

CHAPTER FOUR

Below the Deck

Action Sequences & Behind the Scenes

Everyone's had the experience: watching TV with someone who pops out to make a cup of tea and returns two minutes later with an irritating 'What have I missed?' The reply is often an offhand 'nothing much' or 'The hero fell over' or 'Shut up and sit down and you'll soon find out.' No-one ever says that a campaign involving twenty-five different departments, hundreds of people, months of preparation, a fleet of vehicles, several countries and hours of filming has been mounted in order to produce two minutes of TV – and you missed it.

In terms of most television productions, that would be an exaggeration – but not in *Hornblower* terms. A two-minute scene really will take all day to film (even a ten-second one will take hours). In the Ukraine, preparation for every scene was doubly difficult because everything had to be translated, and technical terms don't translate well. And as well as the normal film departments, they were dealing with harbour and, sometimes, military authorities. At one point, the script called for a large explosive to be detonated near Sevastopol and, as Andrew Benson says, 'The authorities are going to want to know about it.'

Indeed they did. Sevastopol is the City of Russian Naval Glory and, while part of the Ukraine, is still the base of the Russian Black Sea fleet as well as the Ukrainian navy. It held out at the Battle of Sinop during the Crimean War and it wasn't about to surrender to another bunch of Brits in a boat.

But even after translating, there is always another problem in the former Soviet Union. One of the legacies of Communism is that no-one is prepared to accept responsibility for anything. Martin Saville, overseeing the building of the models in Petrozavodsk, recalls that it took three weeks for the shipwrights to grasp the concept that he was there to guide them – and to take the flak for anything that might go wrong. In Yalta, another crew-member requested a stick for driving the cattle that

Filming the rescue of Simpson from the wreck of the Justinian *– a classic example of the difficulties of shooting at sea.*

were being loaded during the sequence at Oran. This was greeted with dark looks and deep suspicion, a long and convoluted conference and, finally, an answer: 'Niet.' It was not possible to have a stick. Further and tortuous probing revealed the reason: they did not have a drawing of a stick from the art department. That department was several miles away and was frantically busy with some of the 229 drawings of everything from the complex blueprint for the pontoon to the dolphins and foliage that grace the *Grand Turk*. Nevertheless, draughtsman Matthew Robinson obliged and drew a picture of a stick which was then couriered to Yalta.

This is not meant to sound like a cheap little jibe at Ukrainian lack of initiative. It's merely illustrative of the fact that initiative is an unfamiliar concept in a country that is still creeping out of the shadow of its totalitarian past towards a very uncertain future. It's also another example of the extraordinary and unexpected difficulties that faced the *Hornblower* team.

More familiar were the difficulties encountered after every department had done its bit and the unit was on set and ready for the day's filming.

Cannon fire is achieved by way of a 'woofer': a machine that compresses air and sends out splinters of cork all over the ship. Woofers can be used at relatively close range without endangering the cast and crew.

On the poop deck, Pellew and his officers survey the action on the main deck, as does the photographer from the forecastle deck. Another example of the limited amount of space on the Grand Turk.

Scene 131 of 'The Even Chance'. This is where Hornblower and his men pull survivors from the sea and, to Hornblower's horror, one of them turns out to be his old tormentor, Jack Simpson. Script-wise, it's just over one page long. In transmission terms, it's about one minute. It took twenty-five people, four boats and three hours to film. The longboat (the only boat actually 'in' the scene) contained the actors, the director and other members of the crew. The camera crew were in a dinghy; the stunt co-ordinator and some wreckage (not the same thing) were on another and a rowing boat stood by with two other crew. The scene was filmed about three hundred yards out from Artek harbour in early November and it had to be in the can by 4.30 p.m. at the absolute latest because of fading light.

Shooting at night on the Black Sea. This is intercut with scenes shot at night with the models at Pinewood. The result: night-time in the Bay of Biscay.

It very nearly wasn't finished. With the problem of positioning the boats and keeping them still, deciding on exactly how the director, sound recordist, director of photography, camera operator, focus puller and stunt co-ordinator – let alone the actors – were going to be able to work together without falling into the sea took hours. Furthermore, it proved difficult to co-ordinate the position of the sun and the boats with the direction of the wind and the increasing swell.

And then some of the wreckage did what it would have done in real life and floated away. More was brought by the third assistant director and make-up chief – the latter glad of the chance to get out to the scene to tend to her artistes. They were towed half-way by a harbour tug; then they had to row the rest of the way in order not to disturb the sound recordist.

That was a relatively easy scene to film.

More complex, and again involving little boats out on the open sea, were several scenes that ran together at the beginning of part four of the same episode. The *Marie Galante* has sunk, and Hornblower and his men are with her French crew on a jolly-boat (effectively a lifeboat) heading, rather optimistically, for England. The crew, had they actually been in the Bay of Biscay rather than the Black Sea, could quite easily have sailed to England in the time it took to film: three days. It is, however, nearly a ten-minute sequence and shows the jolly-boat adrift at sea, at dusk, in the early morning and at night.

Andrew Grieve remembers 'being cast adrift in a small rowing boat with fourteen people while everyone else was hovering around in inflatables. You couldn't move [nor could anyone go to the loo] for twelve hours a day. It was extremely tiring – especially for the cameraman, Steve Murray. He had the camera on his shoulder the whole time.'

Make-up chief Christine Allsopp remembers it as being terrific fun – at first. 'It quickly became known as the grumpy-boat,' she adds. 'And it was a prime example of everyone mucking in.' To keep the boat as steady as possible, they lashed it to the inflatables which were in turn steadied by oars – and whoever happened to be in the right place wielded those oars. Make-up person, medic, mechanic or actor: it was a case of all hands on deck.

On film, there may only be one little lonely boat bobbing around on the high seas, but in reality there was a flotilla of craft jostling against each other.

Probably the most technically difficult sea-based scene to film in the whole series was the fire-ship scene in Gibraltar harbour. Filmed live at night in the Crimea and with the model ships at Pinewood, everyone involved remembers it as convoluted, complex and, at times, frightening. It's a long sequence, covering five pages of script (*Hornblower* scripts run to an average of 110 pages). In the Crimea, three cameras were used – most scenes need only one – and one of them actually melted in the heat. In the normal course of events, this would have meant that the camera crew would have burned to death. The unlucky camera, however, was a bolex, the cinematic equivalent of an aircraft's black box. It's left to its own devices – in this case it was shoved out into the path of the fire-ship – and runs without a crew. Like the black box, its contents will survive almost any disaster. The camera was a write-off, but the film remained intact.

Director Andrew Grieve (far right) prepares to film the sequence where Hornblower and his men are adrift at sea for three days in a jolly-boat (the boat below). 'It's like playing some terrible kind of three-dimensional chess in your head ... dealing with the wind, tide, sun, the angle you want to shoot at and taking into account the reverses at the same time ...'

Amanda Lean is the script supervisor on *Hornblower*. The title is something of a mis-nomer: she is, in effect, in charge of continuity. It's her job to time everything, to liaise with everyone behind the camera before they go into rehearsal, to time the actual take and make sure all the action and dialogue has been covered. 'You could say,' explains Amanda, 'that I'm the last person at the end of the line before the camera rolls. I should be saying "Are you all happy?" before we begin the scene.' Andrew Grieve overhears this and bursts out laughing. 'You made me very unhappy this morning. Twice.'

But Andrew's unhappiness is always fleeting: Amanda has worked with him before and, on *Hornblower*, has stood behind the camera with her stopwatch and her clipboard for every day of filming throughout the entire shoot. 'What people don't realize,' she says, 'is the number of set-ups involved in filming a scene.'

Set-ups – positioning the camera for a take – are painstaking procedures. To an observer, it's an agonizingly slow process to watch. Yet this is the means by which, on television, it looks as if the camera is running about filming the action as it happens. Nothing could be further from the truth.

'Take the scene in episode four,' says Amanda, 'when Moncoutant comes out of his house, shoots Fauré the mayor, sees a boy singing the *Marseillaise*, goes to shoot the boy, is thwarted by Mariette and Hornblower, then turns on his heel and walks back up the steps to his house.'

A simple scene, surely. The script says it all takes place outside Moncoutant's house during the day.

'Yes,' says Amanda. 'But what it doesn't say is that it involved seventeen set-ups and took us from 8.00 a.m. to 4.30 p.m. to film.'

It gets worse. 'Action scenes,' says Andrew Grieve, 'are incredibly boring to film. Actually, I shouldn't say boring . . . I don't *mean* boring [he does] . . . I mean they're just terribly painstaking. You have a shot here of men's feet; another one there of a gun going off; then you have a sword-fight, then people running and muskets going off. Paradoxically, an emotional scene, one where actors are hardly moving at all, is far quicker. Action scenes, from behind the camera, just involve an inordinate amount of little bits of stuff that has to be pieced together.'

Andrew Benson is more blunt. 'There's no such thing as an action scene. All the action takes place in the editing.'

Cue Amanda Lean and her clipboard. 'The scene in episode four when they land at Muzillac . . . it's actually three short scenes pieced together.'

Oh yes. Looks simple enough on the script: one page and one line. Only fifty-three words of dialogue.

'It took three days to film,' says Amanda, 'and involved the greatest number of set-ups we've ever done. Thirty-two – with three cameras. It took all morning to film seven words of stage directions.'

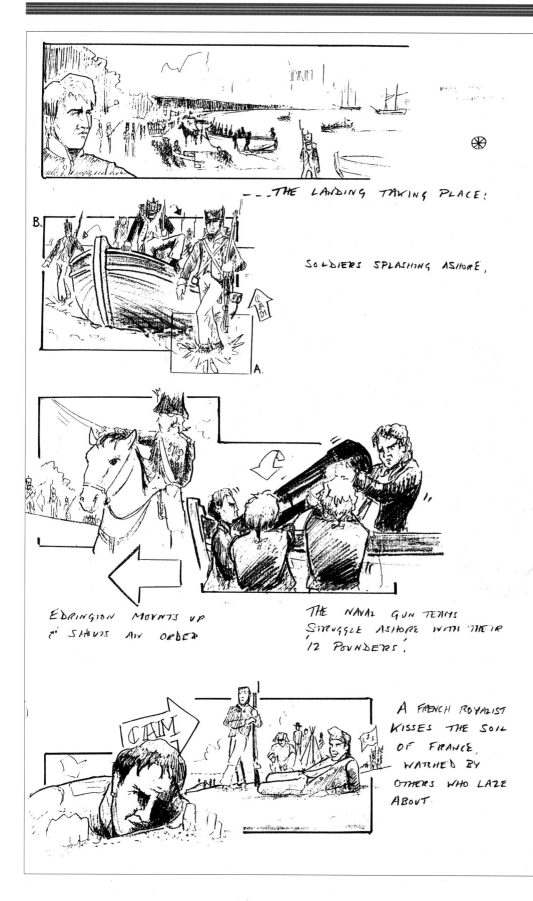

---THE LANDING TAKING PLACE:

SOLDIERS SPLASHING ASHORE,

EDRINGTON MOUNTS UP
& SHOUTS AN ORDER

THE NAVAL GUN TEAMS
STRUGGLE ASHORE WITH THEIR
'12 POUNDERS',

A FRENCH ROYALIST
KISSES THE SOIL
OF FRANCE,
WATCHED BY
OTHERS WHO LAZE
ABOUT

Storyboards for the landing at Muzillac. Sketched by the director Andrew Grieve and drawn by a storyboard artist, they detail every angle, character, wide-shot and close-up. 'It's as if I've already shot the scene in my head,' says Andrew Grieve, 'months before the camera starts to roll.' These are just a few of the storyboards drawn to illustrate the seven simple words of stage directions. Some pictures may paint a thousand words – but here it's the other way around. 'The entire landing force is now ashore' is a simple thing to write, but a complex operation to film. It took an entire morning.

Looking at the footage just completed – a definite contender for 'It'll be Alright on the Night'. Robert Lindsay's hat has just been blown to the other side of the ship by an over-enthusiastic woofer (air cannon).

So woe betide any budding scriptwriter who pens the words 'the entire landing force is now ashore' if he doesn't know what that simple phrase entails.

'That scene,' says Andrew Grieve, 'was the most difficult of any of the land shoots. There were fifty people in each boat. Twenty of them were rowing. They've been trained but they're not experts, and if they'd ended up sideways on an Atlantic roller they would have had it. Thankfully, we found a lagoon to film at (the beach at Troia in Portugal). Even so, the problems of people jumping off boats into several feet of water as they came ashore could have been pretty nasty. It's quite a big jump – several feet into the water – and they were all carrying equipment.'

'Three days,' interjects Amanda. 'And three cameras – including a bolex.'

A bolex of the non-melting variety, as it turned out. The little camera was buried in the sand, quietly filming the horses and men as they stampeded across the sand above it.

MAKE-UP

'It's not just about a wig and a powder-puff' – *Christine Allsopp, make-up and hair designer*

On set, make-up designers are some of the first to start work. Likewise on pre-production; for make-up designers in period drama are amongst those responsible for creating the 'look' of the piece. Long before the actors have been cast, the make-up chief will be familiar with the characters, the scripts, the ideas of the director and costume designers; he or she will have budgeted down to the last hairpin and – in this case – sent thirteen trunks of supplies to the Ukraine because there's no way on earth you can buy so much as a wet-wipe in Yalta.

Christine Allsopp, chief make-up and hair designer for the Ukraine episodes, explains some of the problems their research threw up. 'In the 1790s long hair was still in vogue in the navy. Shorter hair was *beginning* to come in – but the majority of men, and certainly the older ones, would have had long hair.'

So that, presumably, meant wigs.

BELOW Off-duty wigs. INSET Make-up continuity shots. Every take and scene has to be carefully numbered and photographed. What appears as continuous action on film may in reality be two sequences shot in different months and in different countries. One continuity slip-up and an actor's hair could grow an inch in half-a-second . . .

Christine looks aghast at the thought. 'No. Real-hair wigs for such a large cast would have been too expensive in time, money and maintenance. The extras, who don't do close-ups, are wearing off-the-peg acrylic wigs [called, incidentally, 'Fionas'] and even then we tailored them as much as possible to suit the actors' faces. But the principals have hair-extensions.'

These extensions, initially, were something of a talking point. They don't come on and off at the drop of a hat (or a wig) but are painstakingly woven into the actors' existing hair and, generally, remain there throughout the three-month shoot. 'It's exactly like having real, long hair,' says Christine with a smile. 'And you have to look after it as if it's your own. The boys soon discovered all about "hair-washing nights". The extensions look incredibly real as well. A visiting photographer asked Christine how long it had taken Robert Lindsay to grow his luxuriant locks. 'Six years,' she replied, before letting him in on the secret.

There are other, less obvious issues for the make-up department to face. One is bearing in mind the sensibilities of the audience and, in Britain, the 9.00 p.m. watershed. With a programme transmitted between eight and ten, make-up has to go easy on the gore on a scene to be shown before the watershed. And, because scenes are not shot in the same sequence as they appear on the screen, a wound has to be photographed once it has been applied. For what looks a single sequence on the screen may be two scenes shot three weeks apart – you need the photograph to ensure continuity.

And on a crowd-scene day you have to get up at 4 a.m. in order to have upwards of one hundred and thirty actors and extras ready for the 6.30 a.m. call time. Seven make-up artists (four recruited locally) will spend anything from seven to thirty minutes on each actor, and then accompany them on set; a set where make-up, like every other department, had to jostle for space. 'It was a pain not having a make-up room on board the ship,' admits Christine, 'but there was nothing you could do about the restricted space. Everyone else had the same problem.' A problem exacerbated, surely, by the fact that the entire set kept moving up and down as well as side to side. 'Yes,' remembers Christine, 'it was quite a challenge fixing wigs and doing make-up on a bouncy castle.'

And an even greater challenge when they swopped the bouncy castle for one of the smaller boats.

Make-up artists are never far from the camera. Christine Allsopp 'does' Ioan Gruffudd's face.

Veyatie MacLeod, make-up artist for the Ukrainian episodes, heads the department in Portugal. On the set at Muzillac for the 'Frogs and Lobsters' episode, unflagging in the 90 degree heat, she's slapping sun-tan lotion on her soldiers from the 95th Infantry. Some of them are looking mutinous, but Veyatie is undeterred. 'They were called Lobsters on account of their scarlet tunics,' she explains, 'not their faces. We've had to spend about £400 on sun-tan lotion, and we've armed all the principal actors with factor 30.'

And do they use it?

'Oh yes,' she says with a laugh. 'The producer's room overlooks the swimming pool and he's been known to lean over his balcony on their day off and shout at them. Actually, we've "coloured them up" a bit so if any of them are a bit naughty we have a bit of leeway.'

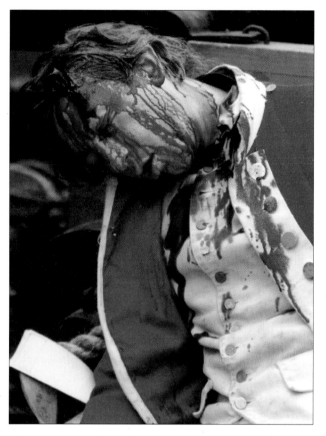

This poor fellow won't be seen until after the nine o'clock watershed – but he's had to spend most of the day with sticky gloop all over his face. No wonder he's tired.

Then she adds that it's the dust, not the heat itself, that is the biggest problem on the mainly land-based locations in Portugal. The landscape is extremely arid, the dust blows all over everyone's faces and clothes and sticks in their wounds. 'But apart from that, we've been very lucky with our extras (and there are many more of them here than in the Ukraine). In the Crimea, they nearly all had close-cropped hair so we needed all those synthetic wigs. Here, most of them have long hair anyway. And,' she adds, 'most of the Spanish and French (of the Hornblower period) had facial hair – as do a great many of the extras – while the British didn't. If we were in the early 1800s, it would have been a completely different style. The collars of the British became higher, making their pigtails stick out at right angles to their heads, so they cut them off – and facial hair came in again.'

Finishing with her Lobsters, Veyatie then picks up her script to double-check the characters for the next scene. There's only one principal artist, the Marquis de Moncoutant, alias Antony Sher – and he's about to be sent to the guillotine. 'The director wants scratch-marks, grazes, lots of blood and the odd prod with a bayonet: he wants him to look as if he's been half-torn apart by the mob.' So Veyatie, a one-woman mob, rushes off with her heavy make-up case into an afternoon where the temperature reaches 100 degrees.

Later, she's asked if she gets tired working long hours in such intense heat. 'Oh but we're not working particularly long hours,' she protests. 'We [make-up] usually start at around six and we're often finished by eight at night.' Veyatie Macleod is utterly charming, but an outsider would be forgiven for thinking she must be mad to work such long hours six days a week. Mad – or totally committed.

THE MODEL UNIT

Welcome to Lilliput, Buckinghamshire. For here, at the Paddock tank at Pinewood Studios, is where Hornblower's adventures meet Gulliver's travels.

It's a strange sight: a giant paddling pool filled with the model ships made in Russia; a horizon that is actually a painted screen; a camera floating about in a fish tank; outsized desk fans that make waves and wind; and men in wet suits, standing chest-high in the water and pushing the boats around. There's something faintly ridiculous about it – but there's nothing remotely funny about what these people are doing.

This is where sequences involving several ships are being filmed by a company called Effects Associates, to be intercut with live sequences shot in the Crimea or in Portugal. Scenes that were filmed on the open seas on the *Grand Turk* will merge seamlessly with . . . well, scenes of men pushing model ships around a tank. But no-one watching the completed film will ever know (unless, of course, they read this) that scenes like the Spanish fire-ship attacking the *Indy* in Gibraltar harbour were filmed half in Crimea in 'real' scale and half in Lilliput. The only clue is that if you can see real people then the scene is 'real'. (Or sometimes half-real: there are things called composite shots, more of which later . . .) For there are no miniature people to play with – although the Russian builders experimented with, and quickly rejected, the idea of using puppets. There are only miniature ships: the fire-ship itself, like most of the miniatures, was twenty feet long.

Surreal scenes on the Paddock tank at Pinewood. The giant fan is a computer-controlled wind machine that creates both wind and waves.

The mechanics of the tank are strangely primitive. The ships themselves are positioned by the men in wet suits and they 'sail' by means of an underwater cable attached to a tractor-like vehicle outside the tank. If the tractor moves one way, a ship moves the other. The wind machines that create both wind and waves are computer-controlled to give exactly the force required, and, with the tractor, create the crucial difference between filming here and at sea: here the ships, like actors, can actually be directed and are not at the mercy of the tide.

The weather is a different matter. Both Martin Gutteridge, director of the Model Unit, and director of photography Roy Field concur that the weather, and the wind in particular, is the greatest hazard. A layman could be forgiven for thinking that achieving realism is a bigger problem – it seems more than faintly ludicrous that models in a tank could appear on television as ships in the thick of battle. But these men have spent their lives distorting reality: Roy Field has specialized for forty-six years in visual effects and was awarded an Oscar for making Christopher Reeve fly in *Superman*.

The water problem in the tank is one of scale. Water in a tank that measures 200 by 250 feet is never going to have the majestic swell of the Atlantic Ocean or the Black Sea. And the waves created by the wind machines are always going to move far too quickly for the scale of the models. Small waves are generated by the wind machines; 'white horses' are created by bouncing waves off the walls of the tank and back against each other; a

Chest-high in the tank, the camera operator asks for direction.

wave machine will create storms – but in all cases the water tears along at a rate hopelessly at odds with the scale of the models. To correct this, they alter the speed of the film in order, as Roy Field says, 'to keep the water heavy and make everything nice and slow.'

The scale of the models also affects the gunfire in battle scenes. To keep to miniature scale, cannons have to be fired at a speed that someone memorably described as sounding like 'a demented elf with a sub-machine-gun'. That, however, is not a problem: the final music and effects soundtrack will be added later.

But now there *is* a problem: they're preparing to film the *Indy* coming into Gibraltar harbour and suddenly a man appears on the horizon. He's half the height of the *Indy* and they're going to end up with a very peculiar piece of film if he stays where he is. Apart from anything else, his presence gives away the fact that the horizon is false: there's a gap between the edge of the tank and the painted backdrop that is the sky. The gap is essential for filming purposes: when they film the tank 'floods' at the far end and the water pours over the lip. Without the gap, the water would lap against the horizon, ruin the impression of a wide open sea – and probably stain the sky with a nasty damp patch.

The man disappears and they begin to film. Given that what they're filming is meant to slot into footage completed months ago in a country no-one here has even set foot in, their task seems rather daunting. Andrew Grieve, director of the main unit, has prepared detailed storyboards for every sequence – intricate drawings that show exactly what is meant to happen when. Additionally, they have the footage they're working around. 'We're very fortunate,' says Martin Gutteridge, 'in that we're fitting these shots into a movie that's virtually finished, so I have continuity on everything. I can go and look at the cut film any time I want to see if it was foggy that day, what the sea was like and exactly what time of day I'm trying to recreate.' So, as long as there are no more pedestrians on the horizon and the men in wet suits remain out of sight, the sight of the *Indy* charging down a tank in pursuit of a tractor will become instead a majestic arrival in Gibraltar.

THE MODELS

The eleven models, ranging from four-and-a-half to seven metres in length, are as spectacular as the *Grand Turk* itself. They are also seaworthy, with fully operational and incredibly intricate rigging – and two miles of cordage in each one. And, apart from some of the deck fixtures (which are never seen on camera) they are historically accurate in every detail. The admiral of this fleet is Martin Saville, who supervised the entire building operation during a five-month exile in Petrozavodsk – the place where Peter the Great built the Russian navy.

The ship-builders were experts, with long experience of building full-sized square-rigged vessels. It took five men anything from five weeks to three months to build each miniature. By the time they had finished, they had three fire-ships, three versions of the *Grand Turk/Indefatigable*, two of the *Julia* and two smaller frigates to play French, Spanish and other British vessels. The largest model, weighing a ton, is of the 74-gun *Justinian*. The differing scales are to achieve perspective in the tank.

The models under construction in Russia. After completion the entire fleet had to be dismantled and ferried across Europe to the tank at Pinewood.

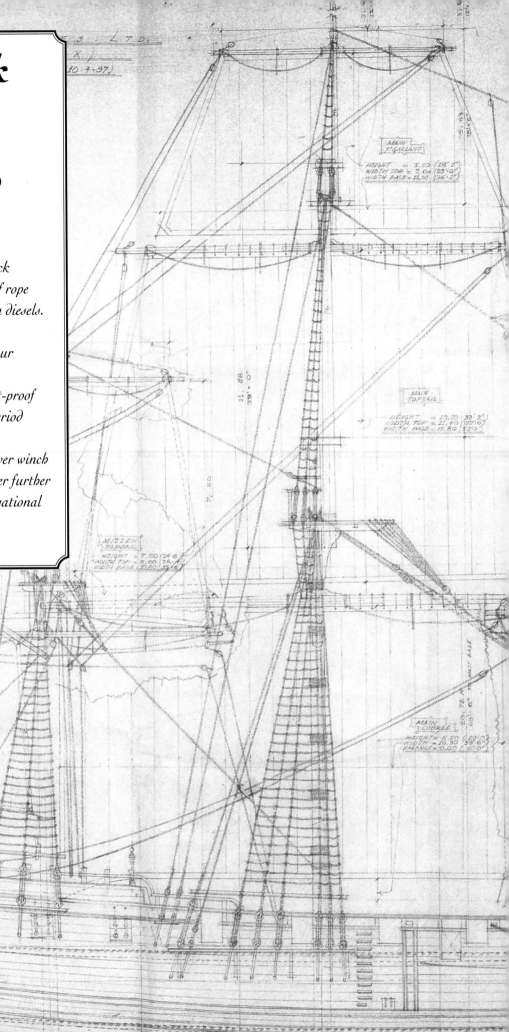

Grand Turk
STATISTICS

- *Built of 250 cubic metres of iroko*
- *Weighs 314 tons*
- *119 feet long (152 including bowsprit)*
- *34 feet wide*
- *Mainmast 117 feet above the water, foremast 117 feet, mizzen 90 feet*
- *Yards 60 feet across and 12 inches thick*
- *Rigging contains more than 3 miles of rope*
- *Powered by two 450 horsepower Kelvin diesels. Carries 23 tons of fuel*
- *Bow thruster and winches driven by four 75 kva generators*
- *22 working sails made of Duradon rot-proof canvas, authentically rigged for the period*
- *10 knots under sail*
- *Concealed in the forecastle are the power winch and upper deck fire pump. A flag locker further conceals her engine controls and navigational equipment*
- *Requires a sailing crew of 26*

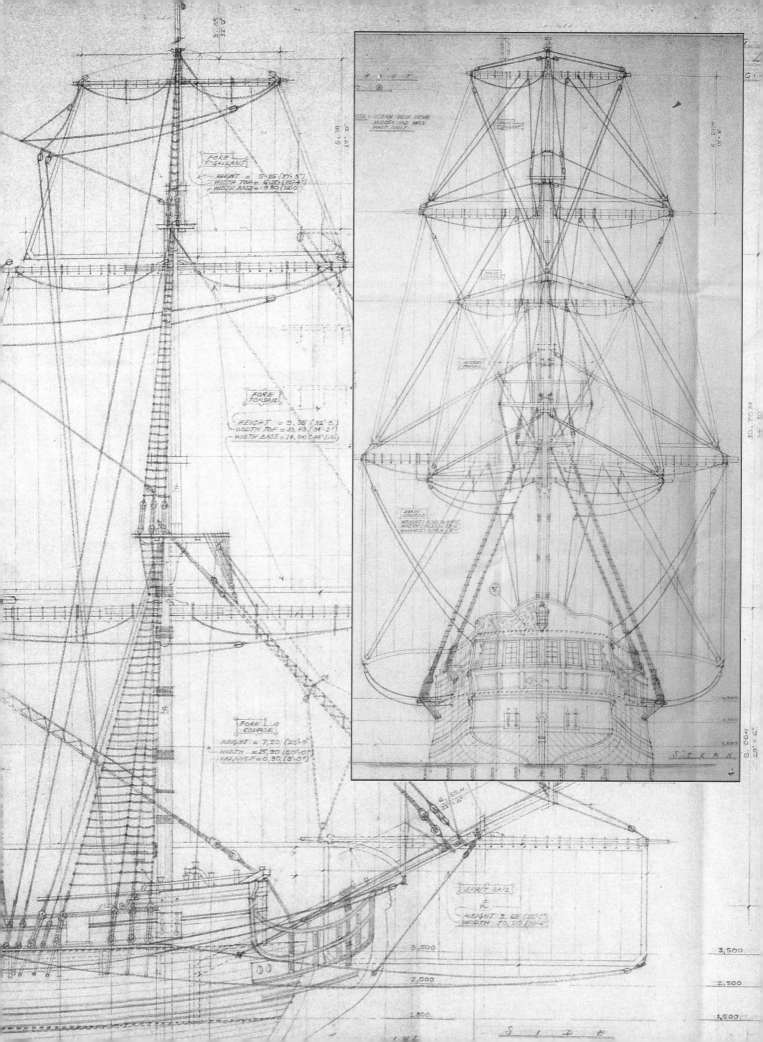

FORE
T'GALLANT

HEIGHT = 5.25 (17'-5")
WIDTH TOP = 6.20 (20'-4")
WIDTH BASE = 9.80 (32'-0")

FORE
TOPSAIL

HEIGHT = 9.95 (32'-6")
WIDTH TOP = 10.40 (34'-2")
WIDTH BASE = 14.90 (48'-1½")

FORE
COURSE

HEIGHT = 7.20 (23'-6")
WIDTH = 15.20 (50'-0")
VALANCE = 0.90 (3'-0")

NOTE - STERN VIEW SHOWS
MIZZEN AND MAIN
MAST ONLY.

MAIN COURSE

HEIGHT 9.30 (30'-8")
WIDTH (BASE) 15.40
VALANCE 0.65 (2'-0")

S T E R N

SPRIT SAIL
&
HEIGHT 3.68 (12'-0")
WIDTH 10.20 (33'-6")

S I D E

3,500
2,500
1,500

3,500
2,500
1,500

Looks can be deceptive. This scene was shot on the Pinewood tank. In the edited film, it's intercut with scenes shot with real people and real ships in the Crimea.
A clue to spotting models is that there are never any people on them — although the Russian shipwrights did experiment with puppets.

COMPOSITE SHOTS

Composites are old cinematic tricks. The technique of what is effectively superimposing frames on top of each other has been used for years — most commonly to turn a handful of people into a crowd. In simple terms, it's like filming twenty people at one end of a room, jumbling them up a bit and filming them in the middle and then doing the same at the other end. By sticking the shots together you end up with sixty people filling an entire room. In *Hornblower*, the landing scene at Muzillac beach was filmed in this way, creating an instant army out of only 150 people.

More complex are the composites marrying live shots with model shots. One of these comes at the very beginning of the *Hornblower* saga, when our hero arrives on board the *Justinian*. That scene, where he introduces himself to Lieutenant Eccleston, was filmed on the pontoon at Artek harbour in the Crimea. The ships in the background, however, are the models in the tank at Pinewood: the two have been composited together.

This technique is straightforward enough — unless the actors move and cross the 'matte line' where the two pictures are joined. That and any subsequent movement reveals or conceals more of the background and creates the need for different images — but only two have been filmed. So new images have to be 'painted' into each frame to keep the movement fluid. As the camera turns at twenty-five frames per second, hundreds of new images may need to be painted in. Until relatively recently this process was both expensive and time-consuming — and generally beyond the budgets of the television community. Now computer technology has advanced to such a degree of sophistication that painting is no longer necessary. And nor is a budget prohibitive. There are numerous composite sequences of live and model action in every *Hornblower* episode.

ASSISTANT DIRECTORS

Looking at the crew list for *Hornblower* – or indeed for any film or television production – it's fairly easy to work out who does what. There are no mysteries about the titles Special Effects Technician, Production Accountant, Camera Operator or Production Designer. The plot begins to thicken, however, when it comes to the assistant directors. There are three – challengingly entitled first, second and third – and they all have differing and clearly defined roles, none of which involve hanging around Andrew Grieve asking if there's anything they can do to help.

David Mason, first assistant director (AD) on *Hornblower*, is responsible for breaking down the scripts into the order in which they will be filmed. With two episodes being filmed at the same time, that effectively means juggling with 250 scenes, several locations, hundreds of people, the weather, travel times, actors' availability, the scripts themselves – and then coming up with a formula that translates into a workable shooting schedule. Depending on any of the above factors, scene 1 of a script may be filmed on the same morning as scene 131. On the other hand, it may be filmed several months later in a different country.

That is usually part and parcel of any first AD's job. Shooting for weeks on end on a boat is not. 'It was a bit trial-and-error on the ship at first,' admits David, 'as it was something of an unknown entity. We just didn't know how much filming we'd get done each day. I mean, you're planning to film a battle at sea, but by the time you've got the

First assistant director David Mason (wearing glasses) listens to director Andrew Grieve discussing his skiing holiday. The 2nd AD is land-based while the 3rd is behind the scenes on the ship.

ship out there the wind has changed, the boat won't go where you want it to, the sun's in the wrong place, they [the ship's crew] will say we'll have to go south-west and travel so many knots till we can stop the ship. Then they have to untie all those bits of string and we're sitting there saying "Does that mean we can start now?" But no,' he remembers with a laugh, 'that's when people started being seasick.'

Despite the fact that David makes scheduling a shoot sound like pinning the tail on a donkey his script breakdowns, even on those first trial-and-error days at sea, were remarkably accurate.

Filming on land poses other, more familiar problems. 'I have to try to get an idea about travel times to and from each location, and the particular difficulties of that location. If it's in the middle of nowhere you think great, no interruptions, no motorways to get in the way. Then you realize that you can't get any of the trucks close by precisely because it *is* in the middle of nowhere.'

Then there are the last-minute changes. Each day's scenes are itemized on a callsheet, but that doesn't mean they're written in stone. If the weather changes, if they're over-running, if an actor is ill . . . if, if, if . . . then the schedule will change. 'That,' says David, 'is when I call Giles and say actually it's all changed and can you get me fifty-two French peasants by the middle of this afternoon?'

The word 'call' is a clue to David's identity. All assistant directors charge around calling each other up on their mobile phones shouting things like 'get me the rubber axe-man'. But it's lunchtime and there's no need for David to call Giles Butler, the 2nd AD. He's sitting beside him, looking mutinous.

'If David does that to me – which he does, a lot – it means I'm taking everyone else by surprise.' And Giles really does mean everyone else. He's the man responsible for compiling the daily call-sheet which usually runs to several pages and details where every single member of the cast and crew are required to be at any given time – as well as how they're going to get there. 'On specifics, I'm working a day ahead of David. On the more general stuff, like mobilizing extras, horses and every facility from drivers to caterers and loos, I'm usually working several days ahead.'

If Giles's job sounds like a logistical nightmare, spare a thought for the 2nd AD on the Oscar-inundated *Gandhi*. The call-sheets for that epic were reputedly the longest in history, running to tens of pages and, one memorable day, included the words 'lunch for 25,000'.

Lunch for 350 seems bad enough, but that's the least of Giles's problems. There have been several late changes to the actual scripts on *Hornblower*, necessitating last-minute schedule changes. 'The worst was in Yalta. At one point it was suddenly decided that an actor with a . . . shall we say *distinctive* profile should be seen on the *Julia* as it sailed past the *Grand Turk*. The actor had gone back to England so David called through, telling me to get a double within an hour. I drove around the streets of Yalta, found this poor bemused guy walking his dog and practically pulled him into the car. I don't think he had a clue what was going on, but he loved it so much he stayed for lunch.'

So that'll be lunch for 351, then.

Luckily for the *Hornblower* crew, Giles speaks fluent Russian. 'It's easy enough to find extras in places where they have agencies. Lisbon has a few, so you advertise, have big casting sessions and off you go. In Yalta it really did get to the stage when I was driving around hauling people off the streets and asking them if they wanted to be in the movies. If you need something or someone at the last minute, you have to get them any way you can . . .'

Then Giles's mobile rings. It's Alex Gibb, the 3rd AD. He's practically impossible to pin down as he, more than anyone else, seems to rush around for fifteen hours a day with a phone clamped to his ear. This particular phone call concerns three falling peasants who are due to die that afternoon but have mysteriously disappeared.

'Alex is generally looking after the set for me,' says David. 'Getting the actors in position, organizing the background action and telling Giles how everything's going on set.'

Not very well, by the sound of things. Then Alex calms down. All is well in the peasant department. They've been found having a siesta in the pigsty.

Alex also has the unenviable task of calling for silence on set every time they go into a rehearsal or for a take. This is a most peculiar and rather enlightening spectacle to watch. Half the people on set wait for everyone else to stop talking. Then, assuming no-one else will hear them because silence has descended, they turn and start whispering to their neighbour . . .

Simon Sherlock (Oldroyd) examines the storyboards for the forthcoming scene. Every single sequence is sketched by the director and drawn by a storyboard artist – often weeks in advance. Storyboards are effectively the templates upon which shooting is based.

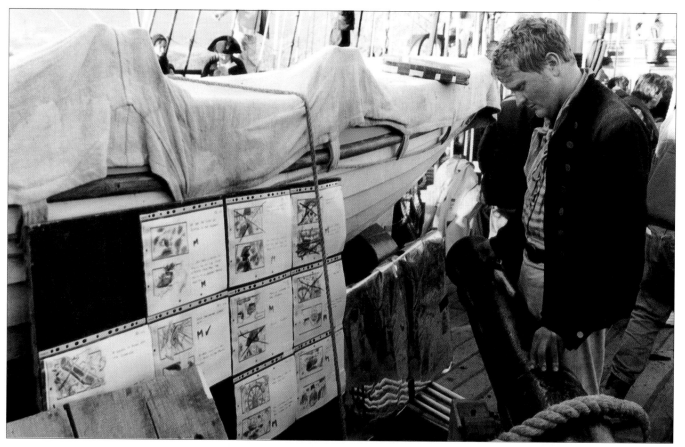

CHAPTER FIVE

Nelson's Navy

Historical Reality

'Nor could I think what world I was in, whether among spirits or devils.
All seemed strange; different language and strange expressions of tongue . . .'

While these words could easily apply to life on a film set they are, in fact, the first impressions of a new boy at sea more than two centuries ago, from *Ramblin' Jack: The Journal of Captain John Cremer, 1770–1774*. For seamen – like film crews – have always been objects of curiosity, living in an enclosed world on the fringes of society. The ancient Greeks, taking rather an extreme view of their seafaring population, debated whether to count them amongst the living or the dead.

C. S. Forester knew of the detachment from society and of the rigid hierarchies of that separate world, and much of the appeal of the Hornblower books lies in the realistic depiction of life in the navy. As well as accurately capturing the minutiae of life at sea, Forester remained true to the broader historical perspective. The backdrop to Hornblower's exploits is always factual – so much so that Hornblower's life is popularly supposed to be based on that of Nelson himself. Another school of thought proposes Admiral Lord Cochrane as the inspiration. A third theory backs the lesser-known Admiral Sir James Gordon as the 'real' Hornblower. Given that Forester himself never volunteered any information on the subject, the most plausible theory is that Hornblower is a composite character whose exploits are based on documented incidents in the lives of several admirals and sea captains, including the above. Rather than recreating the life of any one individual, Forester borrowed from the lives of many.

In the filming of *Hornblower*, however, the producers recreated Forester's creation as far as possible. Yet, as Andrew Benson points out, 'We're making a drama and not a documentary. This is 1998 and we have to make a few compromises – but we endeavour as much as possible to make it convincing to a wide audience. To convince people dramatically is the overriding concern.'

Mr Midshipman Hornblower (Ioan Gruffudd) and Captain Sir Edward Pellew (Robert Lindsay).

UNIFORMS

Oddly, there is much about naval life at the time that, if portrayed on screen, would look like dramatic licence rather than historical accuracy. The question of dress is one such example: the idea of a naval 'uniform' only evolved in the mid-eighteenth century, and only applied to commissioned officers and midshipmen. Yet even in the nineteenth century, there were captains who paid for their officers' uniforms and dressed them as they liked. As late as 1820, the Captain of HMS *Harlequin* dressed his crew up as . . . harlequins. Yet most captains were not so flamboyant nor, probably, rich enough to indulge such whims.

Officially, naval uniforms were introduced in 1748. Legend has it that they were inspired by the Duchess of Devonshire's riding habit of a blue coat with white lapels but, as the costume designer on *Hornblower* says, 'I think that's probably an apocryphal story!'

And he should know. For the costume designer is John Mollo, author of several books on uniforms and Oscar-winning designer for the costumes for both *Star Wars* and *Gandhi*. He is also a lifelong fan of the Hornblower books. In short, he is the person best qualified to design the thousand-odd costumes for this production.

Together with wardrobe supervisor Gordon Harner, John Mollo started research on the *Hornblower* uniforms many months before filming. 'Initial research involves studying paintings from the period,' explains John Mollo. 'Then we move on to individual sketches for each character.' 'Sketch' is something of an understatement: each drawing is a work of art in its own right, detailing everything from the buttons on a midshipman's coat to the buckle on his shoe. And some characters are drawn several times: midshipmen and officers had two uniforms, the 'dress' and the 'undress' uniform.

Costume department drawings flanked by, left, Hornblower's uniform and, right, Pellew's. These were their 'undress' or working uniforms. They also had more elaborate dress uniforms.

The details on all the costumes are intricate and, vitally, true to the period. The black Hanoverian cockade on an officer's bicorne hat ('more of a fashion statement than a practical hat'); the white patches on coat collars denoting the rank of midshipman ('which are still worn today'); the gold lace and brocade on dress uniforms – everything, as John Mollo explains, reproduces the look of the period.

And then the costumes, from French peasant to Moorish treasurer, from Spanish admiral to English captain, had to be made. 'I designed the costumes for the *Sharpe* series (also filmed in the Crimea) and was conscious of the wear and tear involved,' explains John Mollo. 'We wanted to own rather than hire these ones, so we looked into the possibility of having them made in Turkey.' This, however, was not to be and so John turned to Angels and Bermans, the largest theatrical costumiers in England.

Because they have been responsible for providing costumes for every conceivable type of drama (including films about the French Revolution) Angels already had many uniforms in stock. Others were made to John's specifications and all had to be tailored to fit the actors and, perhaps more important, the exact period. Given that modern film-making allows little time between casting actors and starting filming, the former consideration could have been a problem. 'We were lucky,' says John Mollo with a chuckle, 'that most of our cast were slim. Their uniforms came from stock and were fitted on set.' Only once were they caught on the hop: one actor didn't fit any stock uniform and a new one had to be made from scratch – on set and in three days flat. And only two actors, Ioan Gruffudd and Robert Lindsay, had their uniforms fitted in London.

Then there is the problem of making the uniforms look old. Brass buttons, gold braid and lace are toned down with French enamel varnish. The white moleskin breeches and waistcoats are, fortunately, washable and break down quite quickly to

The Spanish captain, played by Frank Rozelaar-Green, on board the Grand Turk. *Spanish uniforms, like the Spanish court of the time, were relatively sober and formal.*

look older. And the woollen coats didn't need a helping hand: exposure to the elements weathered them and, in some cases, shrank them. 'When actors fell into the sea,' John Mollo reveals, 'we did have occasions when uniforms shrank quite considerably.'

Then there are, as John reveals, the more 'filmic' aspects to consider. 'When you're designing a film you have to bear in mind the colour scheme – that nothing must stand out too much to distract the attention of the viewer. A classic case of this,' he adds with a grin, 'was on *Star Wars*. On my first meeting with George Lucas he said he didn't want to notice any of the costumes.' (One gets the point, but is there anyone who *didn't* notice what Darth Vadar was wearing?)

'On set,' continues John, 'it helps to look at everything through half-closed eyes to make sure that nothing stands out – particularly if it's too white or too bright.'

Any viewers on the lookout for anachronisms will find one where whiteness is concerned. In the episode entitled 'Frogs and Lobsters', French *émigré* marines, escorted and accompanied by their British counterparts, land at Quiberon to stage a counter-revolution. They are dressed in pre-revolutionary white uniforms. In the source book, *Mr. Midshipman Hornblower*, Forester has them dressed in blue. In reality, their uniforms would have been the same colour as those of the British: red. Resident in Britain, they would have been outfitted by the British. But, as John Mollo points out, 'We put them in white to make them stand out and be instantly recognizable from the others.' It sounds eminently reasonable and, given that they would have worn white prior to the revolution, perfectly feasible.

Months later, the landing has taken place and, on the set at Muzillac, John is watching his troops with a critical eye. A republican soldier walks past, gulping Evian water. But it is his strange helmet that catches the attention. It looks like that of a Roman legionnaire, and there's a band of fur round it. Artistic licence?

'Oh no,' says John. 'At that time the French troops were obsessed with anything classical. These particular helmets were especially popular with the Maréchal de Saxe, who took a great interest in the excavations at Herculaneum in the 1750s. And around that time French uniforms were also influenced by countries on the borders of Europe like Hungary and Croatia, where everything was a bit wild and with bits of fur all over the place.'

While the helmets predated the revolution, adherence to the Bourbon white lasted until Louis XVI's execution in 1793. 'For the first few years the uniforms were something of a mixture of old and new. The red, white and blue of the Republican uniforms was first worn by the Garde Nationale de Paris, combining the arms of Paris with the Bourbon white.'

OPPOSITE *The costume supermarket. The entire wardrobe department has to move to where the action is. It was housed in this marquee for eight days before moving lock, stock and barrel to the next location.*

Then Antony Sher, playing the Marquis de Moncoutant, emerges from make-up. He looks uncannily like Widow Twankey. 'Well,' says John, 'Moncoutant is meant to be a rather extreme character, so it's fitting to rouge him up a bit and make him slightly theatrical.'

But the *hat*?

'The Widow Twankey thing?' says John with a laugh. 'That's his – to shield him from the sun. The one he wears as Moncoutant is a bicorne – but with a completely over-the-top Bourbon cockade.'

Ah.

As for the Spanish troops encountered in 'The Duchess and The Devil' episode and, briefly, in 'The Examination for Lieutenant', John Mollo says they played it safe. 'The Spanish were an old-fashioned lot, rather sombre. They didn't go in for anything loud.' Then this erudite expert on uniforms breaks into a grin. 'Anyway, we were rather limited by what Angels and Bermans had hanging on the rails . . .'

Given that the four episodes of *Hornblower* span several years and cover three countries, and that uniforms (not to mention the actual *Hornblower* scripts) were constantly

Antony Sher as the flamboyant French émigré, the Marquis de Moncoutant.

OPPOSITE *Hornblower in his working uniform with his faithful division of seamen: Finch (Chris Barnes), Styles, (Sean Gilder), Oldroyd (Simon Sherlock) and Matthews (Paul Copley). Seamen didn't have designated uniforms. These ones don't have christian names either.*

evolving, the odd minor anachronism may have crept in. Yet this is a drama, not a documentary, and it would not be reasonable – or financially feasible – to cater for even a relatively minor change in the appearance of uniforms for the sake of one line of text. If *Hornblower* were expected to replicate the navy in every detail it would have to be – as the Royal Navy almost certainly was – the largest industrial concern in the world.

Behind the grand considerations of researching and creating one thousand costumes lie the more mundane aspects of a film wardrobe department. Filming on location – especially when that location is the Crimea – means taking *everything* with you. And everything has to be itemized. The wardrobe department shipping list runs to thirteen closely typed pages and makes for some pretty arcane reading. There are two scissor tuners, 147 pairs of shoe laces, freezer bags (?), various types of glue, 83 kilos of fuller's earth (for cleaning uniforms – they would have used it in Nelson's day as well), boot jacks, torches, stationery, bobbins, brasso and bin-liners. There are ironing boards, heel grips, shoe polish and starch, candles, cotton buds, pimping cord, poppers and paint. And then there are the clothes . . .

NAVAL HIERARCHY

The uniforms worn by officers and midshipmen differentiated them from the rest of the ship's company – and served as a reminder that they were the only ones with the all-important social distinction of the right to walk the quarterdeck. For naval hierarchy was largely a microcosm of British social life, and everyone knew his 'place' in shipboard society. In the broadest possible terms, there were four major hierarchies within a ship's company: officers, ratings, marines and servants. Yet within those categories were a myriad other distinctions, some of them ill-defined, that illustrated the one important difference between the navy and society in general: people rose through the ranks.

The position of a midshipman like Hornblower illustrates this curious amalgam of official rank and social reality. Midshipmen occupied a limbo between the ranks of officers and ratings: officially they were the latter, in reality they were officers-in-waiting and were expected to behave accordingly. Officially they were inferior to warrant officers such as the armourer, sailmaker or cook, yet in reality a warrant officer could be court-martialled for striking a midshipman as if he were a superior officer.

Midshipmen were often, but not always, young gentlemen – and some of them let power go to their heads. In *Hornblower*, one such midshipman is Jack Simpson in 'The Even Chance'. While no longer young (most midshipmen were between the ages of fifteen and twenty-two, although some were as old as fifty-five), he uses his position to bully the seamen in his division and vents the spleen of his thwarted ambition on the younger midshipmen. There are plenty of contemporary accounts of midshipmen 'furnishing pretexts to get seamen punished' and 'kicking a man about the thighs and body'.

This is one way to stop cheese from going mouldy: these provisions are made from polystyrene.

FOOD

Although there are enough surviving accounts to dispel the popular myth that equates life at sea with a floating concentration camp, no-one ever claimed it was a picnic.

On land, providing food could be a problem, but if a squadron was at sea for any length of time, it was impossible to carry bread, fresh fruit or vegetables. Breakfast on land would consist of bread and cheese: at sea it came in the rather less appetizing shape of burgoo (a mixture of oatmeal and water) or 'scotch coffee' (bits of burned bread boiled in water and sweetened with sugar). Yum.

There were always barrels of salted beef and pork ('stony, fibrous, shrunken, dark and gristly' according to one account) on board ship, but for the majority of a ship's company fresh meat at sea was a rarity. Officers, however, often had the means to supply their own foodstuffs, turning their ships into Noah's Arks in the process. Their meat couldn't have been fresher: cattle, sheep, pigs, goats, hens and geese would have been running around on deck only hours before they were eaten. Some animals were kept as pets: in exotic seas monkeys, parrots and bears were not uncommon and there is even one account of a French battleship with an elephant on board. But for the men, fresh meat – in the form of fish – was only in regular supply in inland waters, supplemented on the open seas by the occasional dolphin, tortoise or seabird.

CATERING IN THE CRIMEA

People on film sets take food for granted. It's always there; there's masses of it, the quality is consistently good and the variety satisfies both the committed carnivore and the lettuce lover. And if it does begin to pall then there are always the hotel restaurants in the evening.

But not if you're filming in the Crimea.

Yalta is a summer resort and, while the gigantic Hotel Yalta remains open all year, its many restaurants close their doors with the onset of autumn. In winter there are few guests – and there's even less food. The Ukraine is impoverished, all food is seasonal and the country's infrastructure does not run to refrigerated transport.

It's a wonder that the catering department manages to feed upwards of two hundred people without resorting to burgoo and weevily biscuits.

Catering manager Becks Burge is remarkably sanguine about the difficulties that face her team. They have to be up at 3.00 a.m. to cook breakfast; they have to shop (sometimes search) for food; they have to transport elevenses, lunch and tea out to the *Grand Turk* and then they have to have another meal ready for the end of the day's filming. Added to that, they have to cater for both British and Ukrainian tastes. 'I suppose,' says Becks, 'we do work the longest hours. I managed to clock up ninety-three hours in one week.'

And yet the food on set was always good, plentiful and varied.

'The only really big problem,' explains Becks, 'is that there aren't any big supermarkets, so you have to go to so many different shops. There's only one that does the sort of rice we're used to – and it's right out of town. That means a forty-minute round trip. Just for rice. And chicken is another problem: you can only buy legs, not breasts – and they come from the Czech Republic.'

'But,' adds Becks, 'it's amazing what I've managed to dig up. I get all excited and buy a shop out of something and ask them to order more but . . . well, it doesn't always happen. And apparently someone spotted corned beef in a shop but they can't remember which one. I can't find it,' she finishes forlornly. 'But I'm desperately trying to.'

Becks may have failed in the corned beef department, but she has scored a big success elsewhere. Every meal consists of a wide variety of hot courses, salads, vegetables, fruit and puddings, and, because lunch has to be taken out to sea, all this has to be packed into hot-boxes and survive a forty-minute journey in an inflatable. 'That means you can't do things like chips,' explains Becks. 'And you have to work around plastic cutlery so you can't have things that people would need a steel knife to cut.'

She could have added that they have to work to as tight a schedule as the film crew. Time and tide may wait for no man, but no man is prepared to wait for his lunch. And unlike the seamen in Nelson's navy, they don't have the on-board alternative of animals to slaughter. (That, at least, is the official line . . .)

These people may look like they're saying goodbye to their lunch, but it's quite the opposite. The dinghy bearing hot-boxes has arrived and they're watching the perilous process of loading them on to the Grand Turk.

Rats were a perennial problem at sea – they can't act. This shrinking violet was never at ease in the role of his aggressive ancestor.

RATS

As well as the food animals, there were also less-welcome creatures on board ships. 'Rats, scorpions, centipedes and all manner of venomous animals devour us.' (quoted in M.E.Matcham, *A forgotten John Russell: The career of a purser and naval officer in the 1730s and 1740s*).

While rats were a problem in that they carried disease and were also perfectly capable of gnawing through the sides of ships, they were, when freshly killed, considered something of a delicacy in the midshipmen's mess. On long voyages they were also an important supply of fresh meat. While the cast and crew of *Hornblower* eschewed poached rat in favour of less exotic game, they did encounter them – with rather unexpected results . . .

Episode one, 'The Even Chance', called for a scene involving rats scrambling about trying to leave a sinking ship (the *Marie Galante*). The rats employed on set, however, belied the image of the ferocious vermin of naval yarn: they were tame, well fed and had no intention of scrambling anywhere. 'They were so bloody tame,' said a member of the crew, 'they just sat and cleaned themselves.' Several attempts were made to encourage them to run towards the camera – all of them fruitless. Either the rats continued their ablutions or ran the wrong way. In the end, the crew sent to shore for a cat to chase them. The ruse worked – but not as anticipated. The cat took one look at the rats and ran away. The rats gave chase, running towards the camera and thus, eventually, to their successful television debut.

Yet rats haven't entirely changed their habits since Nelson's day. One, uninvited and untamed, crept aboard the *Grand Turk* in the dead of night and headed straight for the ship's cabins. 'At 3.00 a.m.,' says Topsy Toner, wincing at the memory, 'I had this excruciating pain in my right toe . . . there was a rat hanging off it with his teeth sunk in.' A grim little episode – with an even grimmer aftermath. 'Of course, when I told everyone in the morning they all burst out laughing. Little did anyone know how serious it was.' On advice from the on-set medic, Topsy had to go to hospital for a course of rabies injections in his stomach. 'Ten days in a row,' remembers Topsy. 'And then more on the twentieth and thirtieth days.' But then in Nelson's time, he could well have been dead by the twentieth or thirtieth day.

HYGIENE

Rats apart, hygiene was a constant problem in the navy in Hornblower's day. The living conditions for the majority of the ship's company were extraordinarily cramped: each seaman had a mere 14 inches of space for his hammock. (In practice, this meant 28 inches since the occupant of the neighbouring hammock would be on watch while the other was sleeping.) The constant damp was another problem and, when a ship was at sea, the gunports in the lower decks had to remain closed, plunging most of the ship's company into permanent twilight.

In 1777 the Admiralty decided that ships should be healthier: special air vents were incorporated into the design of new vessels and hospital ships were assigned to the fleet. Until then each ship's 'hospital' was the surgeon's cockpit, a grim little hole where operations would be performed with the aid of rum, a leather gag, candlelight and boiling pitch to cauterize amputated limbs.

Then, in 1810 the Admiralty went one step further and issued soap as part of a ship's rations.

While hygiene was obviously not an issue during the filming of *Hornblower* (although there were a few wrinkled noses on the subject of nautical plumbing: two chemical loos in the forecastle deck) there were problems with damp. Several actors' uniforms shrank after their escapades in the sea and, like everyone else, they spent much of their time on board being cold and wet. Due to the hotel's haphazard heating system, they also spent rather too much of their time on land in the same condition . . .

Below decks on a man-o'-war — the sanitised version. The reality would have been far more cramped, with lower deckheads, more people and — if they really were about to fire the cannon — rather less chit-chat.

PRESS GANGS

Press gangs have, in fiction and film, had a rather bad press. They are depicted as the legal equivalent of highwaymen, terrorizing the countryside at times of war and forcing all able-bodied men into the navy. While this undoubtedly happened in some instances, the reality was more complex and usually less brutal. Pressing was conducted by the Impress Service, an organization that dealt with all forms of recruitment (including volunteers), straggling and desertion. While they did raid inns to recruit seamen, most of these were near coasts and rivers, where they would be most likely to find men who knew about working on ships and boats. Until Prime Minister William Pitt introduced the Quota Scheme in 1795 (stipulating a certain number of recruits from each English county and port), it was highly unlikely for non-seafaring men to be pressed. It was, after all, in the interests of the navy to recruit men who were, if not exactly willing, at least able.

No-one, of course, was press-ganged into taking part in the filming of *Hornblower*, or even forced to do anything he didn't want (although there was a rumour, vehemently denied from on high, that the one-legged actor who appears as an amputee in episode one started the production with two . . .).

An artist's impression of a Hornblower *casting session.*

PRIZE SHIPS

Prize ships were an important feature of war in Nelson's time, and feature prominently both in Forester's books and in the television production. By capturing an enemy battleship or merchant ship and sailing it back to an English or neutral port, the victorious crew stood to make money. Most of the value of the ship and cargo would be shared among the captain and crew. The captain received the lion's share but an ordinary seaman could, if he were lucky, earn more in an hour from prize money than he could from years at sea. Theoretically, huge sums could be made but in reality an ordinary seaman was more likely to earn around £10 from a good prize. Not bad compared to a wage of 24 shillings per lunar month. For ship's captains it was a different matter: some of them – the real Pellew included – made great fortunes from prize money. (The treasure ship *Hermione*, captured in 1762, netted the biggest single prize ever taken by British crews in the eighteenth century – more than £500,000.)

Prize ships of war were eagerly sought by the Admiralty: they made for an extremely cheap way of building up the navy. As there was little, if any, difference between a British ship-of-the-line or frigate and its French counterpart, a change of ensign and crew was all that was required to make the vessel switch sides.

As far as filming was concerned, this was a godsend: it enabled the *Grand Turk* to masquerade as the *Papillon* as well as playing the leading role of the *Indefatigable*.

A prize ship turns into a booby prize as Hornblower's first command goes disastrously wrong.

79

The Ship's Company

Interviews with the Cast

The most notable liberties taken in the filming of *Hornblower* are with the characters. None has been invented for the purposes of filming, but all have been expanded to provide both consistency and drama. For, as well as action, television audiences demand well-rounded characters. As producer Andrew Benson puts it, 'The danger of concentrating on battles and explosions is that you end up saying "That's all very well but who are the characters?" I think most people still watch television drama to see well-drawn characters as well as a story well told.' Others in the production echo this: everyone involved in creating the look of the piece – the costume designers and make-up artists as well as the director and the actors themselves – made great efforts to develop and differentiate each character. Forester only elaborated on one of them – Hornblower himself.

> He would be a gangling and awkward man, because that would be an effective contrast with his mental ability . . . He was not going to be an utterly fearless man: as he was going into danger he must recognize it as danger . . . He obviously must have the indefinable good looks that a woman would notice and yet which he himself would underestimate . . . besides being self-conscious he would be shy and reserved . . .

In recounting the genesis of his hero in *The Hornblower Companion*, C.S. Forester reveals the hugely detailed picture he had created in his mind. Hornblower, he goes on to explain, would be a 'man alone', beset by self-doubt, hugely self-critical. (The christian name Horatio, Forester reveals, was inspired by *Hamlet* and not Nelson.) He would also be an accomplished mathematician, he would be tone-deaf, he would be afraid of heights and, throughout his career, he would suffer from seasickness.

Forester actually created Hornblower in mid-career. The first Hornblower book – in order of writing and publication – is *The Happy Return*, where Hornblower is introduced as a married man in the throes not only of war but of a passion for Lady Barbara Wellesley, fictional sister of the Duke of Wellington. From the outset, Forester started as he continued in marrying fact with fiction. The Duke of Wellington was an accomplished violinist; his father a composer of minor distinction; it would be likely that Lady Barbara, had she existed, would also be musical. And that's why Forester made Hornblower tone-deaf: it would add that essential ingredient to romance – a barrier between the couple. Another, more substantial barrier was erected in the shape of Hornblower's marriage – a loveless one upon which he had embarked in a spirit of misplaced honour.

Then, with the backdrop of the demise of the Spanish South American Empire decided upon, Forester said to his publisher that he would call his hero Hornblower. 'When we parted,' Forester reminisces, 'he [Michael Joseph] was very little wiser and far more alarmed than before we met.'

He needn't have been alarmed, for the rest is history – a history that has seen Hornblower rise to the rank of fiction's favourite naval hero.

Hornblower strips off to investigate the damage to the Marie Galante's hull. The scene had to be shot several times – not much fun when it's winter in the Black Sea.

IOAN GRUFFUDD *as Hornblower*

Fiction's favourite naval hero has spent half the day in the cold embrace of the Black Sea. His most gruelling scene yet, checking the damage to the hull of the *Marie Galante*, has been completed. Now the director has two more minutes in the can – and Ioan's repeated immersions have left him with a sore ear.

There's no mention in Forester's work about his hero being similarly afflicted, but one wouldn't be surprised if that had been the case. For in many aspects of both character and physical appearance, Ioan Gruffudd *is* Horatio Hornblower. He's tall and dark, rangy rather than gangly, he's modest, he's good looking (although he underestimates this), he's hugely generous in his praise of others, he's left-handed – and he even feels slightly seasick every day. On screen, too, he embodies the essence of the reserved, self-conscious yet courageous and determined character he plays.

But off screen there are some telling differences. One is that Ioan is highly musical. Another is that he's Welsh. 'I suppose,' he muses, 'being musical is my Welsh heritage.' So is his name – a source of consternation to some prospective agents when Ioan finished his three years at RADA. They wanted him to change it. But Ioan's name (pronounced 'Yowan', with a short 'o') is like Barbra Streisand's nose. She famously rejected advice to change it – and look what happened to her. 'It's who I am,' says Ioan. 'I appreciate that someone who doesn't speak the Welsh language wouldn't have a clue, but it *is* my name.'

The eldest of three children, Ioan Gruffudd was born in Cardiff where his parents were both schoolteachers. The first time he left home was to go to RADA. Leaving aged twenty-one – four years ago – he walked straight into a role in *Wilde*, playing John Grey, one of Oscar's earlier loves. 'Stephen [Fry] was wonderful,' remembers Ioan, 'really fantastic. But I was terribly nervous the first time I met him. It was for the rehearsal for the scene where we're in bed together . . .' After *Wilde*, Ioan played the part of a young Welsh officer in the film everyone thought would sink without trace. 'I'm the one in charge of the only lifeboat that came back to look for survivors,' he says of *Titanic*.

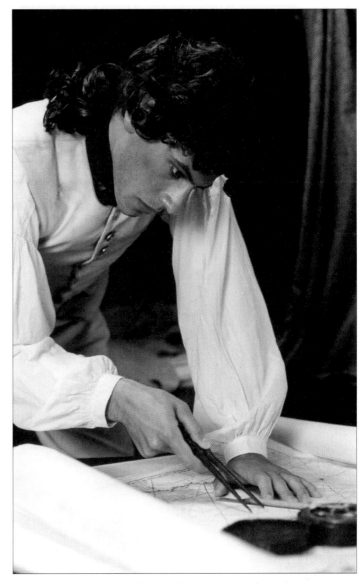

'By making Hornblower a skilled mathematician,' wrote C. S. Forester of his hero, 'I was indulging in shameless wish-fulfilment.' Hornblower's mental agility was one of the reasons for his rise through the ranks.

On returning from filming in Mexico, Ioan went straight into an audition for *Hornblower* and landed the part that most actors of his age would probably scupper a ship to get. 'For someone of my age,' he says with characteristic understatement, 'it's a real treat.'

Only a treat?

Ioan grins. 'It's the best thing that's ever happened.'

For Ioan, it happens nearly every day. Apart from Sundays (everyone's rest day), he has only had one day off in the last three months. 'My admiration for his concentration and stamina,' says Andrew Benson, 'is unbounded. When you're shooting you might be doing scene 1 followed by scene 163, so to work that hard, hold it all in your head and bring it out every time is tremendous. I couldn't have imagined anyone could be that good.'

ABOVE *Bloodied but unbowed. The blood goes by the trade-name of 'Pigs Might Fly'.*

Seven months later, Ioan is sitting in the shade outside his Winnebago on set in Portugal. Everything is different: the country, the comfort and the climate – and so is Ioan. He looks somehow bigger. It takes a moment or two to realize that he hasn't grown in either stature or in girth, but in confidence. As if to illustrate that, he's talking freely about the most striking difference between Ioan Gruffudd and Horatio Hornblower: their ability to express themselves and their emotions. 'The scenes I've just filmed with Estelle [who plays Mariette, Hornblower's first love] were difficult. Hornblower can't put his finger on his emotions, he's gauche and naive – and I felt very uncomfortable in that situation, a bit off balance. It's not me, but it's perfect for the character.'

Ioan looks extremely surprised when asked if returning to play that repressed and tentative character after a five-month break isn't difficult or, worse, merely 'more of the same'.

'No! I'm just as excited about it this time round – perhaps more so. The work is more interesting – you don't have to contend with the ship all the time – and there are more new characters.' Last time round, Ioan said it was 'a privilege' to work with established actors. This time he repeats it again, even though the industry is buzzing with the news that he's now one of the hottest young actors of his generation.

Today, he's extremely hot – it's nearly 100 degrees – but he shows no signs of flagging, even though he's still working six days a week. He's socializing too: he's had a stream of family and friends out to stay in Portugal. 'Well,' says Ioan with a grin, 'it's nice to be able to make the best of somewhere like this. It's a lot more accessible, and a lot more attractive than the Crimea. It's fun.'

And there's the nub of the difference between Ioan and the character he plays. Horatio Hornblower, one feels, would not have been a great deal of *fun* to be with. Ioan Gruffudd is.

OPPOSITE *Hornblower and his first love Mariette (Estelle Skornik).*

ROBERT LINDSAY *as Captain Pellew*

'He was quite a fella,' says Robert Lindsay of Captain Sir Edward Pellew. 'A man who wouldn't give orders for things he wasn't prepared to do himself. There's a famous story about a time when his crew were swimming. Pellew playfully pushed a young sailor overboard, thinking he was about to jump anyway. Then he realized that leaping overboard was the last thing he intended to do – he couldn't swim. So Pellew, wearing full uniform, dived in to save him.'

It's probably that sort of behaviour that inspired Forester to incorporate the real Captain Pellew into his Hornblower stories. Although Pellew would not have been around to captain Hornblower's first vessel (he was already a vice-admiral by the time of the American Revolution), his avuncular attitude to his crew makes him the perfect mentor for the young midshipman.

'I like the relationship between Pellew and Hornblower. He treats Hornblower as a son and that's very important to the piece on a human level. He's aggressive with him, and sometimes abrasive, but he's also extremely fond of him and can see he's going places.'

Robert has encountered *Hornblower* before – under less happy circumstances. 'After I'd got this job, my mother rang me to tell me she'd found an old GCSE paper of mine, based on *Mr. Midshipman Hornblower*. Apparently I'd written that "due to my lack of nautical knowledge I found this book dull and uninteresting". I was heavily into Conrad at the time and found Forester a bit 'Boy's Own'. It's funny coming back to it as a screenplay: I think the scriptwriters have done a wonderful job with the characterization.'

Like most of the cast and crew, Robert hasn't filmed at sea before – but he's acted practically everywhere else. One of British television's best-known faces, he has starred in *Citizen Smith*, *GBH*, *Jake's Progress* and countless other film, television and theatre productions on both sides of the Atlantic.

Hornblower, however, marks another first: problems with the police. 'People in Yalta find it a bit strange that men have pigtails,' says Robert, flicking the luxuriant locks that would have taken him six years to grow had they been real, 'and when four of us went out to eat in town when we first arrived, we realized the police were taking an interest. Sure enough, they later stopped us, got into our car, and tried to arrest us.'

Back in England, Robert's daughter did quite the opposite. 'She took one look at my hair and refused to get into the car with me.' The hair extensions, painstakingly woven into the actors' real hair, remain in situ all through filming, although at one point Robert's were very nearly ripped from their roots and blown into the Black Sea. Captain Pellew and Lieutenant Eccleston are standing on the poop deck of the *Indy*, reeling from the blast as the powder-room of a nearby ship is blown to bits. (In fact it wasn't even remotely 'near by': the battle raging around them took

In real life, Captain Sir Edward Pellew amassed a fortune from prize ships. He was also, as depicted in the series, firm but fair and with an avuncular attitude towards his protégés.

place in the tank at Pinewood Studios three months later.) But the blast itself, engineered by special effects, was rather too near, and there was too much compressed air in the woofer that generated it. As Robert composed himself for one of the most serious scenes in the whole series, the woofer blasted and sent his hat flying straight to the other end of the ship. A short, stunned silence followed – and then the entire crew burst into hysterics. It was several minutes before anyone could compose themselves for a retake; but to no avail. The script required Robert Lindsay to look at once horrified, awed and distraught. All he could do was giggle. It took three takes before it was 'alright on the night'.

'Everybody knew of Pellew's reputation and success,' wrote Forester in Mr. Midshipman Hornblower. *'Distinction, promotion, prize money – an officer under Pellew's command could hope for all of these.' He was also a hard task-master, and Hornblower's promotion to lieutenant didn't come easily.*

ANTONY SHER *as the Marquis de Moncoutant*

'Moncoutant is very juicy: it's great fun doing all this shooting and sending people to the guillotine. They let me shoot someone else today – it wasn't even in the script.' With a wicked glint in his eye, Antony Sher leans back in his seat – placed, fittingly, several feet from the guillotine. On it lies the corpse of a polystyrene peasant whose execution Sher's character, the Marquis de Moncoutant, has just ordered. Moncoutant is without a doubt the most monstrous character in the series, and Antony Sher is delighting in the role.

The malevolent marquis is actually an amalgam of two characters from Forester's original: Moncoutant himself and his fellow aristocrat of the *ancien régime*, the Marquis de Pouzauges. Both were portrayed as bombastic, intolerant and bent on teaching the upstart revolutionaries a thing or two by returning to France to raise an émigré insurrection. And they acted, to a large extent, as one. Now they *are* one. The way the character has developed leaves no room for another like him. He's probably the most extreme character in the series; returning to France, portable guillotine in tow, he expects to be greeted with open arms by his loyal villagers in Muzillac. Quite the reverse happens.

Moncoutant swearing allegiance to the old Bourbon order, flaunting the fleur-de-lys on his collar and sleeve. Already horrified by his arrogance, Hornblower senses disaster ahead.

89

ABOVE *Moncoutant (Antony Sher) meets his nemesis and is carried to the guillotine by the very people he sought to subjugate.*

OPPOSITE *Trigger happy. 'It's great fun doing all this shooting and sending people to the guillotine,' says Antony Sher. 'They let me shoot someone else today – it wasn't even in the script.'*

Moncoutant is meant to be repellent; yet his own tragedy saves him from becoming a posturing caricature of evil: he simply can't understand that he's the author of his own grisly fate under the blade of his guillotine. And he's a character that Antony Sher recognizes. 'I'm from South Africa and Moncoutant reminds me of those mad white South Africans who simply won't change; who refuse to accept that their world is no longer there. They believe – and I'm approaching Moncoutant in this way – that they have a divine right to rule over people; that it is the natural order of things.'

Sher is not so sure that it's the natural order of things for men to ride horses: 'I don't think I'll ever be entirely at ease on horseback. For a few moments you feel comfortable and think, "Oh, I'm John Wayne", but I'm actually a little bit frightened of all animals. I can't speak French either,' he adds with a laugh, 'so there have been moments when I'm neither in control of what I'm saying or where I'm going.'

But Antony Sher is certainly in control of what he's *doing*. One of Britain's most highly regarded theatre actors, he's also familiar to film and television audiences, most recently as Disraeli in *Mrs Brown*.

'I've done more theatre than film, but I find filming quite romantic.'

Doesn't he get bored with all the hanging about?

'No. I rather like it all.'

It would be difficult not to like it all during a day like today. It's nearly ninety degrees under the sun on the set of Muzillac, but there's a soft breeze and cool drink in the shade where Antony Sher is sitting.

The Marquis de Moncoutant, however, is already living on borrowed time. He's going to lose his head tomorrow. 'Yes,' muses Sher. 'I'll be physically under the guillotine – and it's a real one.' Then he turns and, with a flash of the extraordinary eyes that make Moncoutant so awful and Sher so amenable, he adds, 'I hope the people who operate it haven't learned to hate me by then . . .'

CHERIE LUNGHI *as the Duchess of Wharfedale*

Cherie Lunghi looks rather incongruous. She's standing in the baking heat outside a caravan, assailed by the smell of frying chips, glittering with jewels and wearing a ball gown. In the background is the Palace of Calhariz. Much closer, behind her in the lunch queue, is a sweaty man in a singlet.

Then, lunch tray in hand (salad, not chips), she moves off into the tent and finds a place at the rickety trestle table with Ronald Pickup and Lai Riobom, one of the Portuguese drivers. Like all the principal artistes on *Hornblower*, Cherie has her own Winnebago. Like them, she only uses it to rest or go over her lines.

And she has every excuse for resting today. Cherie Lunghi has been based in Los Angeles for the last three years and has been flying back and forth between there, Lisbon and London since she started on *Hornblower* three weeks ago. 'The jet-lag's beginning to catch up,' she confesses. 'It's just as well I'm having an early night tonight.'

But that early night was not to be. No-one lets Cherie Lunghi creep off to bed at an unsociable hour: she's far too much fun to have around. And everyone regrets that she's only around to play a part in one episode – that of the Duchess in 'The Duchess and the Devil'.

Cherie herself has no regrets about her role. 'It's lovely to get something that's playful and humorous . . . slightly comedic. At the same time, I want to make her real as well, not to descend into farce.'

Cherie Lunghi is an actress playing an actress impersonating a duchess. The character calls for a ribald sense of humour, a broad Yorkshire accent and a lot of teasing of Hornblower over his gaucheness and obvious attraction to her. 'It's fun,' says Cherie, 'and although I think I've got an ear for accents, I did a bit of work with a brilliant voice coach.' Her own accent betrays more of the Central School of Drama than of her Irish/Italian parentage.

The role of the Duchess also gives her 'one of my most impressive entrances ever'. She is hoisted on to the ship in an armchair. 'I don't know if that's actually what they did, but it makes sense given the height you'd have to climb from a longboat into a frigate. For a woman in all her petticoats trying to retain her modesty . . .'

Cherie's pretty familiar with petticoats. 'I was all corsetted up for *The Mission* in Colombia – in even greater heat than this. And then there was *The Buccaneers*, *Much Ado About Nothing* [with Robert Lindsay] and, of course, *Frankenstein*. I was his mother.'

Cherie Lunghi hardly looks old enough to be anyone's mother, let alone Frankenstein's. Then she reveals that she has a twelve-year-old daughter who will shortly join her in Portugal.

An hour later, she's called back to set, where, this afternoon in the grand hall of the Palace of Calhariz, she will be outed as an actress and not a duchess. But in real life, Cherie Lunghi could be either: she has the versatility of the former and the grace and poise of the latter.

The enigma: is she or isn't she the person she appears to be?

Denis Lawson as the fearsome Captain 'Dreadnought' Foster in 'The Examination for Lieutenant'.

JAMIE BAMBER *as Archie Kennedy*

Jamie Bamber is lolling about on the poop deck of the *Grand Turk*. The sun is shining, the sea is calm and Yalta, seen from a distance, could well pass for the glamorous resort it used to be. It's a far cry from that day three months ago when, in the middle of a storm, Jamie walked on to the set of *Hornblower*.

'I was completely overawed by the number of things going on,' he admits. 'It was the scene when Hornblower first joins the *Justinian* and I had to deliver these very simple lines – something like "Shoreboat ahoy!" – and then I had to tell him to jump aboard. But the rain machines were on and chucking it down, it was bitterly cold, there was lots of noise, lots of pigs and loose women running around and I couldn't even hear the director shout "Action!" or anything.'

But Jamie must have done something right on his first ever day on a film set. His character, Midshipman Archie Kennedy, was greatly expanded half-way through shooting. He was never meant to appear in the episodes shot in Portugal. As things have turned out, he's become a major player. Jamie puts this down to the fact that he was 'Hornblower's first friend, same age, same rank and everything'. And although Hornblower quickly rises above him, there's 'only a hint of rivalry'.

While it's true that Kennedy was partly developed to give Hornblower a friend (something he lacks in the original) and to lend continuity and further drama to the series, it's also true that Jamie Bamber made things easy for them. He was clearly born to act. After only one year of formal training, he left LAMDA in June 1997, landed the part of Kennedy two weeks later, filmed *The Scarlet Pimpernel* during the break in *Hornblower* and, if rumour is to be believed, is now being considered for several major television roles.

He's bright, too. He speaks fluent French and Italian and has a degree from Cambridge. Is there anything he can't do?

'Plenty of things,' laughs Jamie.

His next words are drowned out by a sudden roar from further down the poop deck. It's one of the Ukrainian extras' birthday, and his colleagues have appeared with a cake. It's placed on top of a convenient box – which later turns out to be a barrel of gunpowder – and then there's lots of back-slapping and present-opening.

The diversion passes and it's back to Jamie. What was he saying?

Jamie grins. 'Can't remember.'

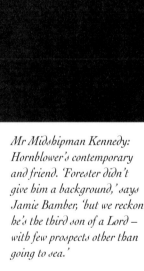

Mr Midshipman Kennedy: Hornblower's contemporary and friend. 'Forester didn't give him a background,' says Jamie Bamber, 'but we reckon he's the third son of a Lord – with few prospects other than going to sea.'

JONATHAN COY *as Bracegirdle*

Jonathan Coy has just spent his day off 'doing' Yalta. It may no longer be *the* summer spot for the smart set, but there's still a considerable legacy from its ritzy past. Czars and aristocracy built palaces here; it was prime dacha territory for the upwardly mobile of both czarist and soviet days – and even now lesser mortals still flock to the various sanatoria to sample the curative powers of Yalta's bracing air.

Fitting, then, that Jonathan Coy should be playing a character with the name of Bracegirdle. Not so fortunate that the place he most wanted to see – the house where Chekov spent the last years of his life – was closed for the day. 'It was *supposed* to be open . . . but then that's Yalta, isn't it? You have to expect the unexpected.'

Bracegirdle, too, has done something unexpected: he's been promoted from a midshipman in Forester's original to first lieutenant in the series. Again, it's a case of an amalgamation of characters. 'He was originally Hornblower's friend and contemporary – a role that Kennedy has rather taken over.' Lest anyone think that Jonathan Coy is miffed by being usurped by Jamie Bamber (who plays Kennedy), the opposite is true. 'We seem to have become joined at the hip. Before the

Lieutenant Bracegirdle. Hornblower's superior officer and friend.

Portugal shoot, we're both off to Prague to film *The Scarlet Pimpernel* (Jonathan Coy in the role of The Prince of Wales), and after that it looks like we might be in the same play together in England.'

Rather than being superseded by Kennedy, Bracegirdle has in fact overtaken him: 'he's something of a mentor to Hornblower, looking out for him. Like Pellew, he takes an avuncular attitude to the young midshipman; unlike the captain, he's in a position where he can be Hornblower's friend as well as his superior officer.' He does things like lend Hornblower clean stockings for his examination for lieutenant, advising him on his appearance and attitude.

Jonathan Coy's own appearance is definitely twentieth century – he's wearing a baseball cap. 'Ah,' he laughs, 'that's to hide my hair. It's a complete pain in the . . . head.' Then he leans closer. 'But don't believe what everyone tells you: some people love having the extensions. You can tell who they are – the ones with the Rita Hayworth look.'

The Rita Hayworth look?

At that moment one of Jonathan's contemporaries – who has complained vociferously about his cranial appendages – walks past with his hair floating around his shoulders. 'That,' says Jonathan, 'is what I mean. Flaunting your locks.'

Hornblower's division were initially extremely sceptical about him: 'His Majesty's latest bad bargain'. Yet they became Hornblower's most loyal supporters.

SEAN GILDER *as Styles*
PAUL COPLEY *as Matthews*
SIMON SHERLOCK *as Oldroyd*
CHRIS BARNES *as Finch*

This disreputable rabble constitutes the division Hornblower inherited from the late and not very lamented Mr Midshipman Simpson. Initially dismissive of Hornblower – 'We thought he was rubbish 'cos he was seasick, even in the harbour,' says Chris Barnes – they soon grow to respect him.

Their characters – Finch (Chris Barnes), Matthews (Paul Copley), Styles (Sean Gilder) and Oldroyd (Simon Sherlock) – have been expanded to lend the series continuity. They were all mentioned in the original, but Forester's seamen were largely interchangeable. Here, they are all different.

'Oldroyd,' says Simon Sherlock, 'is a bit of a wide boy, up for a life of adventure on the high seas. But that's not what it's all about, as he soon finds out.' Simon, like the others, and in collaboration with the director, was encouraged to invent a background for his character to compliment his role in the script. As the youngest, Simon's Oldroyd has turned out to be a volunteer who, in the first episode, is still in his first year at sea. Not surprisingly, he's also

Chris Barnes

Simon Sherlock

Sean Gilder

Paul Copley

the most impressionable. In episode three, when they are imprisoned in the Spanish fort, it's he who sides with Simpson's rebellious replacement against Hornblower.

'Both Andrew Benson and Andrew Grieve,' says Sean Gilder, 'wanted actors who could play strong characters who were all very different but who also got on very well.'

It couldn't have worked better. Despite the fact there is an age difference of twenty years between the four men, they spend a lot of time, on and off set, in each other's company. 'The other day,' says Simon, 'we went with Sean to get some meths for the portable cooker he has in his room. We managed to find a chemist and, instead of serving us, the woman behind the counter dragged us into the back room and plied us with vodka and food. It was brilliant.'

Sean Gilder thinks Styles is 'one of the hardest men at sea. His lines' says Sean, 'are the most cynical. He's a bit of a rough diamond. I definitely picture him as being press-ganged years ago.' Sean himself looks the part. 'I'm six-foot tall, dark and acne-scarred and if I go into a room without smiling I can look pretty scary. Most of my roles bear that out; I've played coppers, soldiers, bent soldiers and coppers who happen to be criminals.' But Sean himself couldn't be more different from the characters he plays. He's one of the most friendly, considerate and erudite people on set. He's also extremely flattering about his fellow actors – and about the scripts that have been honed out of books that he says 'without sounding horrible, are hardly literature. Joseph Conrad is my favourite author and Hornblower, by comparison, is just a series of well-described events. But in the scripts they've made the stories much richer, both in plot and characterization.'

Paul Copley, who used to be a teacher, agrees. His character, Matthews, is the most sanguine of the four, the most loyal to Hornblower, and the most experienced seaman of the quartet. In real life, that's also true. Paul played an oil-rig worker in the ITV drama *Roughnecks* – another part that called for weeks of filming at sea. So filming on the *Grand Turk* can't be too much of a challenge?

'You must be joking. Oil rigs are much easier. They may look like the set of *Alien*, but they stay still. There's no rolling and pitching like you have here.'

Today, the ship is pitching like crazy. Yet these four men are doing what their counterparts in Nelson's day would probably have been doing. They're sitting in the bowels of the ship, chatting, reading, and two of them are playing backgammon. It's hugely atmospheric: they're dressed in character (looking pretty unsavoury) and the ship is making that creaking, protesting sound that only a wooden ship can make. Then they turn to a discussion about the scene they've just filmed: bringing the cattle on board in the episode set in Oran. 'What was so good about it,' says Paul with a grin (Paul, unlike Matthews, has a permanent smile on his face) 'is that it wasn't acting. Like the rowing, it was actually *doing*. That's one of the greatest pleasures of this project. Even if it's not in the script, everyone mucks in, helps each other. Everyone *does* things.'

'Yeah,' says ex-*Soldier, Soldier* actor Simon (who does a hysterical imitation of the Mancunian line producer mouthing off about the Ukraine), 'being in *Hornblower* is dead good.'

DORIAN HEALY *as Simpson*

'I had three absolutely brilliant months. It was a great life experience – not just a job. That doesn't happen very often.' Dorian Healy, who plays Hornblower's tormentor Jack Simpson in 'The Even Chance', is the complete opposite of his character. You couldn't imagine Simpson brimming with enthusiasm about anything unless it involved being vile to someone.

'I loved the Crimea. I found Yalta fascinating and I thought the people were incredibly inspiring ... they're making do with so little. I just loved walking around the place and on my last day I went to Sevastopol and saw all the Charge of the Light Brigade stuff ... it was really quite moving. And the whole experience of being on a boat was brilliant. If I could have come back to England on it I would have. And ...'

And if Dorian Healy runs as fast as he talks he's going to win the New York marathon (he's training for it now). And that's in-between acting – *Soldier, Soldier, No Bananas, Playing the Field* are some of his more recent credits – and writing a play and a film.

Simpson was 'a great character' to play. 'He's more than just a bully. I've tried to give him some more modern neuroses to make him more interesting as a character – and more interesting for me to play.'

He certainly gets some interesting things to do. Dorian spent a great deal of time leaping in and out of the sea for the scene when Hornblower unwittingly rescues him – and then a whole day filming the duel at the end of the episode. 'I found the sea thing really pleasurable. I'm a great water lover and anyway I was wearing a wetsuit under my uniform so it wasn't cold. The only unpleasant thing was diving head first into jellyfish the size of footballs.'

The duel scene was filmed on Bear Island further along the bay from Yalta. A promontory rather than an island, it's also the subject of Yalta's most famous legend. It's supposed to be a giant bear, crouching in and drinking out of the Black Sea, trying to empty it and thus prevent a seaman from sailing out of the life of a local princess (or milkmaid – the myth caters for all tastes) who has fallen in love with him.

Dorian Healy fell in love with the place, not a princess. 'I'd definitely go back.' (Refreshing news indeed – one of his fellow actors said that 'I'd rather have my gall bladder removed with an oyster fork than go back to Yalta' ...)

Dorian is the only principal actor on *Hornblower* who wore a wig rather than hair extensions. 'No choice – my hair was far too short for extensions. But it was a brilliant wig. I can usually detect one from a thousand yards, but I think this one fooled everybody. And it meant that I got my head back every night ...'

Hornblower's tormentor Mr Midshipman Simpson (Dorian Healy). He failed his examination for lieutenant on account of his mathematical incompetence – yet another reason to dislike Hornblower. Dorian Healy was the only principal actor to be fitted with a wig rather than hair extensions.

ESTELLE SKORNIK *as Mariette*

'Papa?'

'Nicole!'

'Bob!'

Few people in the United Kingdom will be unfamiliar with those words, nor with the beautiful, tantalizing – if monosyllabic – creature who has turned the antics of Papa and Nicole into a national obsession.

There's nothing monosyllabic about the ex-model turned actress at the centre of that obsession. Estelle Skornik is rattling along in her native French, talking about her latest role: as Mariette in *Hornblower*. She's quite as ravishing in the flesh as she is as Nicole – even if rather less lavishly dressed in Mariette's simple dress and cap. But it's not difficult to see how a hesitant hero called Horatio has fallen hopelessly in love.

The young schoolteacher who captures Hornblower's heart. 'Mariette,' says Estelle Skornik, 'knows exactly what she wants, and she's prepared to fight for it. Yet there is a conflict in her heart . . .'

Nor is it a departure from the spirit of *Hornblower* to invent a romance that didn't exist in the original (Mariette appears, but there is no relationship with Hornblower). As producer Andrew Benson says, 'It would be totally wrong to make Hornblower into some sort of rampant womanizer. On the other hand, he *is* a romantic hero, so what we've tried to do is to make this episode believable within the context of what we know about Hornblower, and about his future great romance.' That relationship, with Barbara Wellesley, takes place later in his career.

But if Estelle Skornik's career has, in England, been defined by the capers of Papa and Nicole, it's quite a different story in France. 'I've been working as an actress in France since 1991 in both film and television.' Estelle then reels off a string of credits, including *Marquise* with Sophie Marceau and, more recently, her first comic role in *The Grand Slam*. If she seems slightly bemused by her reputation in England, she's the first to acknowledge that 'it's opened doors for me'.

And it opened the door to *Hornblower*, her first time on the British screen in the bits between the adverts – and her first English-speaking role. 'It's not speaking English itself that's difficult [Estelle's English is practically fluent], it's the intonation of the language that's so different. But I worked with a voice coach, listened to a walkman . . . no, it's very agreeable to be acting in English.'

And what of Mariette?

'It's a great part,' enthuses Estelle. 'I really like people with conviction, who defend things close to their hearts. The problem is that Republicanism is close to Mariette's heart, and so is Hornblower, who represents the other side. It's a real moral dilemma.'

But there's no dilemma for Estelle herself on the set in Portugal. 'English actors,' she says with a grin, 'are such *gentleman*. They're so gracious. And everyone here's really straightforward, so willing to lend a hand.'

There was no shortage of people to lend a hand when Estelle, jumping out of

The source of the conflict. The mutual attraction is strong – but the loyalties are wrong. Whether he likes it or not (and he doesn't) Hornblower is firmly aligned with the French émigrés. Mariette, on the other hand, is fiercely Republican.

a window with Hornblower as they made their escape from the village of Muzillac, fell and twisted her ankle. A positive horde of helpers took her to hospital. The next day, hobbling around on crutches, she demonstrates a sense of irony as fine as her command of English. 'They tell me to jump out of a window,' she says, 'and what happens? I twist my ankle. I have to return in a week's time in order to be shot. What do you think will happen?'

I don't know.

Estelle smiles and leans closer. 'I don't trust these people. I think they really *will* shoot me.'

RONALD PICKUP *as Don Massaredo*

'It's much easier doing it in general conversation, without a script. If you just talk away about nothing in particular and don't concentrate too much then it comes more naturally. It all flows much better.'

Ronald Pickup is talking about accents. To illustrate his point, he launches into a monologue about nothing in particular in a Spanish accent that flows naturally, easily and convincingly. With his goatee beard, neatly trimmed moustache and patrician features, he could quite happily pass for Don Massaredo, the Spanish aristocrat whom he plays in episode three of *Hornblower*.

'But,' he adds, 'it becomes much more tricky when you're actually reading from the script. One becomes terribly conscious of playing an accent instead of a person. You can get carried away and start exaggerating the aspirate 'h' and end up sounding like Manuel from *Fawlty Towers*.' As he finishes, Ronald Pickup's accent changes, again to illustrate his point, and you half expect him to don an apron and start spilling wine as he turns into a hapless Spanish waiter.

It's an interesting point, treading the fine line between sounding foreign and sounding foolish. 'And if they're fairly short scenes with elliptical lines,' he continues, '. . . if they don't flow on from each other it can be quite tricky.'

An hour later Ronald Pickup is in front of the camera and one can't help thinking that he was talking a load of nonsense: he makes it look incredibly easy and has reverted to the Spaniard who speaks frightfully good English. Yet he later repeats his remarks about accent versus character, and, like Cherie Lunghi before him, praises the voice coach who helped him.

Don Massaredo, Commandant of the Spanish fort and Hornblower's kindly captor.

Like Antony Sher, he also praises Jordi Casares 'who did the riding. But,' he adds with a grin, 'I *can* actually ride. I think I can ride better than it looks on film. I don't think my horse liked being on the sand today. It bolted . . .'

Ronald Pickup – and the mellifluous, very English tones of his 'normal' voice – is well known in British theatre, film, television and radio. From the National Theatre to *The Mission*, *The Day of the Jackal*, *Amy's View* and *Uncle Vanya* to *Silent Witness*, his extensive range also encompasses comedy, including ITV's *Behaving Badly* with Dame Judi Dench.

Hornblower is 'a joy to be part of. It's like being with old friends. In many ways it *is* being with old friends. John Shrapnel [Charette] is an old friend of mine, I know Jonathan Coy, and Cherie and I are old pals – we'd known each other for years and then we were both in Colombia in *The Mission*.' Ioan and Ronald also have a connection. 'He was at RADA with my daughter.'

It's tempting, if slightly shaming, to pry for gossip. There isn't any. 'No; that's Ioan; he's just like that. It's quite remarkable for someone his age to have such strength and poise – and charm. And it's not as if he's going out of his way to be sweet. His job is to concentrate for twelve hours a day.'

Ronald Pickup does, however, have a grudge against *Hornblower* (the film, not the man.) 'The hair.' He tugs at the offending pigtail. 'I can't wait to rip it off.' Then, looking slightly bemused, he turns and adds, 'I have to admit, being strictly honest, that I've always wished I had more hair. Even when I was younger I wanted more luxuriant locks. But in this weather . . . God no.'

The weather, as the day wears on, grows ever hotter, and Ronald has an awful lot of hanging about to do before his next scene at the end of the day. Doesn't that bother him?

'Not really. I'm maybe not the best at switching off. I wish I could read a book or paint while I'm waiting. But hey,' he adds with a glint in his eye, 'I get *paid* for hanging around. The acting's for free.'

ABOVE *Don Massaredo with a copy of* Don Quixote. *The 'Duchess' has asked him to give it to Hornblower as she thinks he will understand a 'man who jousts at windmills'. Fittingly, the tiled mosaic in the background depicts the story of Don Quixote.*

LEFT *Sam West as Major Edrington in 'The Frogs and The Lobsters'. 'Kindly address me as "my Lord"' he says to Hornblower. But their awkward relationship develops into friendship.*

CHAPTER SEVEN

Mr. Midshipman Hornblower

Synopses of the Four Adventures

All four episodes are based on action described in Forester's second Hornblower book, *Mr. Midshipman Hornblower*. (The first book, *The Happy Return*, introduced Hornblower to the world as a captain, mid-career, in the latter years of the Napoleonic Wars). In *Mr. Midshipman*, Forester went back in time to relate the adventures of Hornblower's first years at sea. In all the Hornblower books, he weaved his fiction around facts, often gleaned from *The Naval Chronicle*, a magazine published monthly from 1790 to 1820 and written largely by naval officers for naval officers.

The series – with the occasional allowance for dramatic licence and with greatly expanded characterization – incorporates all the adventures described in the ten chapters of *Mr. Midshipman Hornblower*, although not in the same order. While episode one covers the adventures in the first five chapters of the book, episode two covers chapters seven, eight and nine, episode three chapter ten, and episode four chapter six.

EPISODE ONE: 'THE EVEN CHANCE'

Spithead, 1794. Under thundery skies and in lashing rain, a seventeen-year-old midshipman takes the first tentative steps of his naval career. Horatio Hornblower clambers aboard the ship-of-the-line the *Justinian* – known to its intimates as 'the good ship Slough of Despond'. 'His Majesty's latest bad bargain,' whispers a seaman of the appalled youth as he looks around the crowded, fetid land-based ship.

It's a baptism by fire. Not only is Hornblower awkward, nervous, seasick and afraid of heights, his peers are wary of his intelligence while the resident bully, Midshipman Jack Simpson, adds the new recruit to his list of targets. A suicidal Hornblower writes to his father, telling him how happy he is.

Simpson beats him up, but Hornblower pretends to his superiors that he 'fell'. The last straw, however, is when Simpson accuses him of cheating at cards, inciting Hornblower to challenge him to a duel – a move that is thwarted by another midshipman who, unbeknown to Hornblower, takes his place – and is killed by Simpson. Simpson, however, still swears vengeance on Hornblower.

When the war against France intensifies, Hornblower and several other men are transferred to the frigate *Indefatigable* which sets sail for the Bay of Biscay. In command of the ship is Captain Sir Edward Pellew, who will become Hornblower's mentor. Simpson remains on the *Justinian* and Hornblower is given command of his division of seamen who initially resent the young midshipman. Yet soon that resentment gives way to respect, for it's becoming clear that while Hornblower is a stickler for detail and duty, he's also kind, conscientious, loyal and honourable – the exact opposite of Simpson.

In the Bay of Biscay the *Indefatigable* captures two French merchant ships. Pellew instructs Hornblower to board one of them – the *Marie Galante* – with a 'prize crew' of four men and sail her to any port in England. Hornblower is thrilled: it's his first command – one that goes horribly wrong. The *Marie Galante* has been holed, causing its cargo of rice to swell and break up the ship. Hornblower, his division and the French prisoners end up adrift at sea in a jolly-boat. And then the prisoners overcome their captors.

Yet Hornblower's resourcefulness saves the day and soon they are picked up by the *Indefatigable*. Hornblower's men now think he's positively heroic; Pellew is quietly delighted with his protégé. Yet for Hornblower himself, the whole episode is but fuel for the flame of his self-criticism. As far as he's concerned, he failed in his mission.

Then the *Indefatigable* is fired on by a French frigate, the *Papillon* – a vessel that has already damaged a British 74-gun ship, ablaze in the distance. The *Indy* gives chase, but loses the *Papillon* in the Gironde estuary. Pellew then gives orders to rescue survivors from the 74-gunner. As they lower boats and race towards the floundering men, the nameplate of the ship floats past Hornblower in the water. It's the *Justinian*, and the first man he rescues is none other than Mr Midshipman Jack Simpson.

OPPOSITE TOP *Our first sight of the young Mr Midshipman Hornblower. On film it's England in midwinter, 1794. In reality, it's high summer in Yalta in 1997.*

OPPOSITE BOTTOM *Captain Pellew casts an appraising eye over the new arrival.*

BELOW *The ship has sunk. Cast adrift in the jolly-boat, the tables are turned as Captain Forget reassumes command.*

'The Even Chance'. Simpson and Hornblower prepare to fight their duel. (An opportunity to compare a wig, left, with hair extensions, right)

Pellew and his officers plan to lower boats and launch an attack on the *Papillon*. Simpson volunteers his services, much to the terror of Midshipman Kennedy, a colleague and now friend of Hornblower's whose life was made a misery by Simpson. He's prone to fits, and Simpson is invariably the catalyst. As they board the *Papillon*, Kennedy is unconscious in the jolly-boat. Unnoticed by anyone else, Simpson cuts him adrift.

Then, in the thick of battle as they struggle to capture the French ship, Simpson wreaks his vengeance on Hornblower. Unseen by anyone except Hornblower himself, he fires up at him. But the shot is a glancing one: Hornblower falls into the sea and is rescued. They are now being fired on from French guns on the shore. Several men are killed and Simpson tries to assume command. Tellingly, he's thwarted by the division he used to command: the men are now firmly behind Hornblower.

Nearby, the *Indefatigable* is under fire from three French corvettes and Hornblower, in command of the *Papillon*, destroys one, and harries the other two into surrender. The *Indy* is saved.

Pellew is hugely impressed and contemplates promoting Hornblower to acting lieutenant. The only stumbling-block is that Hornblower refuses to retract the accusation that Simpson shot him. Pellew is obliged, grudgingly, to allow a duel to be fought. Simpson fires and wounds Hornblower before the order is given. According to the rules, Hornblower is allowed to shoot back at his leisure yet, disgusted by Simpson's cries for mercy, he merely walks away. Then Simpson lunges from behind his back with a dagger but is felled by a lethal musket-shot – fired by Pellew.

An embarrassed Hornblower thanks Pellew for saving his life. Pellew reminds Hornblower that he saved the lives of all aboard the *Indy* and predicts a brilliant future for his protégé. We suspect he's right.

This episode is an amalgamation of the first five chapters of *Mr. Midshipman Hornblower*, the first of which was called 'The Even Chance'. Like the other chapters, it is a self-contained short story set in 1794 and – unlike the others – was inspired by Forester's thoughts of his own mortality. He writes in his *Hornblower Companion* that the idea of a duel occurred to him after he suffered a heart attack. 'Perhaps it had been my own subconscious estimate of my chance of survival . . . it (the even chance) was a phrase which might perhaps apply to a duel.' Forester goes on to explain that the rules and etiquette of a duel were, in fact, directed at eliminating chance. Hornblower may not have known this – and it wouldn't have mattered if he had: he was 'so angry and unhappy that he would risk ending his life if he could put an end to his troubles.'

While the motivation for the duel remains the same in the film, the treatment is different. The story is expanded to incorporate and expand on both the characters and action from the next four chapters, whilst keeping the story within its real historical context. The sequence featuring the *Marie Galante*, for example, is set in the aftermath of the Battle of the Glorious First of June whilst the attack against the *Papillon* borrows from the fact that French ships later crept along the coast from the shelter of one battery to the next, with British ships eagerly seeking an opportunity to attack.

Wounded by Simpson's pre-emptive strike, Hornblower is given leave to shoot back at will.

A study in pomposity. A boat carries a Spanish captain towards the Indefatigable. *The Spaniards have just made peace with France and are therefore no longer allies of the English. They're actually about to become their enemies . . .*

EPISODE TWO: 'THE EXAMINATION FOR LIEUTENANT'

Anchored in the bay of Cadiz, the *Indy* is approached by a Spanish boat. Its rigidly formal captain informs Pellew (via Hornblower's halting translation from French) that Spain has made peace with France, is therefore now neutral rather than Britain's ally and will be entitled, under the rules of neutrality, to fire on the *Indy* if she remains at anchor off Cadiz. A livid Pellew has no choice but to make sail.

Meanwhile, in the Straits of Gibraltar, the above threat is being played out for real: a Spanish lugger has fired a warning shot at a British transport ship. Puzzled by the shot, unaware of Spain's now-neutral status, the captain of the ship advocates surrender. Yet his passenger, the legendary and fearsome Captain 'Dreadnought' Foster, pulls rank, assumes command and fires on the Spanish ship, which fires back.

LEFT *Pellew is openly sceptical of the maverick 'Dreadnought' Foster.*

BELOW *Foster's methods may be unorthodox, but he knows what he wants and he plans to get it.*

The *Indy* later arrives at the scene and finds a wrecked ship, dead men and cattle floating on the surface, and only three survivors – one of whom is Foster. He tells his rescuers that he is en route to resume command of his ship, the *Dreadnought*.

It transpires that Pellew and Foster know each other of old – and that they don't like each other. Hornblower, however, is greatly impressed by Foster – and vice versa. While slightly worried and annoyed about Hornblower's obvious hero-worship of Foster, Pellew nevertheless puts forward his protégé for next month's examination for lieutenant. Foster disembarks in Gibraltar and heads for the *Dreadnought*.

Now that the Spanish have deprived them of supplies, Pellew is obliged to halve all rations on the *Indy*. Bunting sacrifices his meagre ration to Finch, who is suffering from fever – and later dies. Hornblower is distressed at the passing of one of his now-faithful division. Bunting, who served with Finch on a previous ship, is devastated. As Finch lapses into unconsciousness, the men on deck are cheered by the arrival of a supply ship, but the cheers become howls of anguish when the Spanish send a fire-ship straight into its path, destroying it completely.

The essence of Hornblower: resolution with a hint of self-doubt. Forester wrote that 'he wasn't going to be an utterly fearless man . . . as he was going into danger he must recognize it as danger.'

Pellew tells Hornblower they are to accompany another transport ship, the *Caroline*, on a supply mission to Oran. The pompous and pedantic Mr Tapling from the diplomatic service joins them in order to conduct negotiations.

Bunting now appears slightly unhinged. Convinced that the officers are getting more than their fair share of food, he steals some rations from the steward's room. Hornblower catches him and reports him to Pellew who, to Hornblower's horror, makes him run the gauntlet.

When they reach Oran, Hornblower and his division along with Tapling and a handful of marines take a longboat to the jetty. Hornblower is aghast to discover Bunting stowed away under a sail; he's evidently intent on desertion. Yet that discovery pales into near-insignificance beside the next: Oran is in the grip of the plague – and Hornblower and his men have been exposed to the infection . . .

The men must stay in quarantine for three weeks. To this end, and to safeguard the much-needed supplies from Oran, they keep separate from the others by crewing the *Caroline*, loading the supplies of cattle and grain themselves and then heading for Gibraltar in the wake of the *Indefatigable*. Hornblower, now captain of the *Caroline*, passes much of the time with his books, preparing for his examination. Tapling thinks they'll get away from Oran without paying for the cattle and grain. He's wrong. The rest of the men want to stay in quarantine for ever: Hornblower has given orders to slaughter a bullock for food. In sharp contrast, the men on the *Indy* in Gibraltar are eating weevily biscuits and wormy cheese.

When the *Caroline* stops to take on more water, the crew find themselves under Spanish fire, and Bunting seizes his opportunity and flees. He is killed, accidentally, by Hornblower who castigates himself for failing to get through to him.

They return to the *Caroline* to find that Foster and the *Dreadnought* have paid them a visit – and stolen some of their cattle. Hornblower is horrified: apart from the fact of the theft itself, they're still a plague ship.

Three weeks later, back in Gibraltar, Hornblower sits his exam. One of the examining panel is Foster – a fact that renders the already nervous Hornblower completely inarticulate. He is saved from almost certain failure by a commotion outside Admiralty headquarters: the Spanish are sending a fire-ship into Gibraltar harbour.

The men, Hornblower included, rush outside to see the fire-ship heading straight for the *Indy*. Neither Hornblower nor Foster hesitate to leap into a shore-boat, board the fire-ship and steer it away from the *Indy*, saving the entire crew from almost certain death.

Pellew is hugely impressed by Hornblower's courage and tells him not to worry about the aborted exam – he'll be well-prepared next time as he has already tasted the 'bitter brew that is a captain's life'.

These adventures, taken from chapters seven, eight and nine of *Mr. Midshipman Hornblower*, were described by Forester as taking place in January and March 1796. The Spanish galleys, while predating that period, were still in service at that time: even as late as 1800, Admiral Keith captured a galley at the siege of Genoa.

By setting much of the action in the Straits of Gibraltar, Forester was addressing a problem often encountered by the British fleet – the harassment by Spanish ships of British vessels that often found it difficult to sail west either because of westerly winds or periods of calm. (Two-hundred-and-two years later, the *Grand Turk* faced the same problem sailing west from Gibraltar en route to Portugal.)

Sailing to Oran, however, is impossible: it doesn't exist. Forester based it on Algiers.

Bunting (played by Andrew Tiernan) after running the gauntlet. He is looking at Hornblower, blaming him for the horrors he has suffered.

EPISODE THREE: 'THE DUCHESS AND THE DEVIL'

Acting lieutenant Hornblower, assisted by only five men, captures the French sloop *Le Reve* off the Spanish coast. The captain is livid that the youngster has managed to pull off such a feat and Pellew, when they sail back to Gibraltar to join the *Indy*, congratulates Hornblower on the squadron's first successful action in six weeks of blockade against the Spanish and the French. Hornblower is astonished to realize that *Le Reve* is his prize ship and that, after sailing it to Portsmouth, he may make £1000 in prize money – his first taste of riches.

But before that, and far more daunting, comes his first taste of the high life. He and Pellew are invited to dine with the Governor of Gibraltar and his wife.

The prospect of Sir Hew and Lady Dalrymple is frightening enough, but Hornblower hadn't counted on another guest, the extraordinary Duchess of Wharfedale, who teases him about his gaucheness and evident unfamiliarity with high society. Hornblower is both embarrassed and astonished, for the Duchess herself is loud, raucous, vulgar – and has a strong Yorkshire accent.

His acquaintance with her doesn't end with dinner: he is asked to escort her to England – and to take a packet of dispatches detailing all the information about Admiral Jervis's squadron.

The Duchess of Wharfedale – but is there more to her than meets the eye?

Both are awesome responsibilities.

But worse is to come: out at sea, they find themselves in fog in the middle of the Spanish fleet. When the fog lifts, they raise *Le Reve*'s original French colours – but to little avail. The captain of the 74-gun *San Ysidro* realizes they are English and forces them to surrender. It's imperative that the dispatches don't fall into enemy hands, so Hornblower is on the point of throwing them into the sea when the redoubtable Duchess comes up with a better idea: why doesn't she hide them in her skirts? It seems like a good idea – until Hornblower hears the Duchess speaking Spanish to their captors.

But Hornblower's worries about the Duchess being a spy are temporarily forgotten when they are taken to a mainland fort and imprisoned. Another British sailor is already there: Hornblower's old friend and fellow midshipman, Archie Kennedy, last seen adrift and unconscious at the end of episode one. He's in a bad way and, after several escape attempts, has lost the will to live.

Soon there is dissent amongst the prisoners. Some of the men side with Hunter, a midshipman who has always resented Hornblower, in seeking to escape without Kennedy. Hornblower is adamant that they should wait until he gets better.

Then the Duchess, who was supposed to be escorted to Lisbon by her captors, reappears on the scene. It transpires that her escort was thwarted by a battle off Cape St Vincent and 'a dare-devil name of Nelson' and that she has been sent back. Don Massaredo, the Governor of the fort, allows Hornblower to take two hours' exercise with her every day and, despite Hornblower's lingering unease about her integrity, they become friendly. It's quite clear that she sees in him the making of a gentleman. It's also clear that Don Massaredo respects Hornblower and later he invites him to dinner to meet a French army captain. To Hornblower's horror, the captain recognizes the Duchess – as an actress called Katharine Cobham.

Hornblower is now desperately worried about the dispatches. He needn't be. The 'Duchess' manages to allay the French captain's suspicions by cultivating his friendship (yes, *that* sort of friendship). Then she leaves – still with the dispatches – on a Spanish trader that will take her to neutral Portugal. She leaves him a copy of *Don Quixote* as she thinks he'll understand a man who 'jousts at windmills'.

Hunter bullies the other men into escaping and Hornblower has no option but to join them. He also takes full blame when they are captured. Don Massaredo doesn't believe him, but is obliged to punish him as the instigator. It's gruesome: he's kept in a hole in the ground with only rats for company. Eventually he gives Don Massaredo his parole not to escape again and he is released into normal captivity, with his exercise privileges restored to him.

Later he and Don Massaredo are walking on the beach and see a Spanish vessel with a split topsail being blown on to a deadly reef known as the Devil's Teeth. Giving his word not to escape, Hornblower asks for the temporary release of his men in order to rescue the sailors from the stricken vessel. His wish is granted, but Don Massaredo is sceptical. 'No-one,' he says, 'has ever been rescued from that reef.'

By the time they reach the vessel there are only four survivors – one of whom is the 'Duchess'. Again her departure has been thwarted. But the dangerous, night-long rescue takes its toll. The now-contrite Hunter drowns, one of the survivors dies of cold and the 'Duchess' herself appears to be on the verge of death when they themselves are rescued – by the *Indy* . . .

Hornblower insists that he and his men must return to the fort as they are on parole. Pellew notes and admires his new confidence, especially when the 'Duchess' gives him the dispatches and relates the story of their time at the fort – yet he says the men must speak for themselves. They do: Matthews, Styles and Oldroyd return under truce. So does Kennedy. Two weeks later the First Minister of Spain issues orders to release them, but Don Massaredo wryly surmises that Hornblower will be back to plague the Spanish. When he does it will be as a commissioned lieutenant. For, as Pellew informed him just before he chose to return to the fort, he was promoted to lieutenant during his incarceration due to his 'exemplary gallantry in a fire-ship attack on Gibraltar'.

Hornblower may be a prisoner, but he and the Duchess are allowed to spend two hours a day together. He doesn't quite know what to make of her. She, on the other hand, knows exactly what to make of him. She's going to help him become a gentleman. She also knows he's smitten by her – and she's not above a little light teasing . . .

ABOVE AND BELOW
Don Massaredo may be Hornblower's captor, but he's something of a reluctant jailer.

This episode is a greatly-expanded version of the final chapter of *Mr. Midshipman Hornblower*, and it's a good example of how the imperative of characterization and continuity guided the makers as much as the basic story itself. For Kennedy doesn't appear in Forester's original. His revival here lends more drama and continuity to the story as a whole, and gives Hornblower what he sorely lacks in his original incarnation: a friend. (It is also only fair to say that, from the outset, the director and producer were looking for ways to expand the character of Kennedy as they were so impressed with Jamie Bamber, the actor who plays him.)

Of the fort, Forester names it in *Mr. Midshipman Hornblower* as El Ferrol, a place that actually exists. Yet here it has become anonymous for the simple reason that El Ferrol is too far away from Gibraltar to make the *Indy*'s journey between the two places possible in such a short period of time. (Do not let it be said that the producers are inattentive to detail . . .)

Forester writes that El Ferrol was so far from the centre of the war and that overland communications were so unsatisfactory that, during a blockade, the town would languish. The Spanish merchant ship (the one that was driven on to the Devil's Teeth) would, on arrival, have been loaded with badly-needed provisions and it was therefore not inconceivable that it would try to run the blockade in a gale. The fact that she split her main topsail at the crucial moment on her departure was Hornblower's salvation. He 'made instant use of the opportunity presented to him, smoothing not only his path to freedom, but also the path of the novelist who undertook his biography'. Forester, like many of his fans, seemed to regard Hornblower as a real person.

EPISODE FOUR: 'THE FROGS AND THE LOBSTERS'

In London, Hornblower is being fitted for his lieutenant's uniform (and is staggered by the price) and Pellew is being briefed by Admiral Lord Hood on the *Indy*'s next mission – to escort French émigré troops across the channel where they will raise a Royalist insurrection against the Republican government. Pellew is somewhat sceptical about their chances of success – all the more when he learns that the campaign orders of General the Baron de Charette, commander of the émigré troops, have been stolen from a British messenger. Hood tells Pellew not to tell Charette himself about the theft: the messenger may have been the victim of a simple pickpocket rather then an enemy spy.

Three other ships, the *Sophia*, the *Dumbarton* and the *Catherine*, sail with the *Indy*. All are carrying a cargo of French troops, the 'Frogs', and the British infantry – 'Lobsters' – who have been deputed to assist them. The latter are commanded by the prickly Earl of Edrington, who stands on ceremony over his title. Charette, commanding the former, is assisted by Colonel the Marquis de Moncoutant, who is making a highly symbolic return to France. He's taking that handiest of travelling companions with him – a guillotine.

Hornblower notes that Matthews, Styles and Oldroyd resent the Frenchmen and regard them as the enemy. 'These,' he wryly points out, 'are the good Frogs.'

The *Indy*'s destination is Muzillac, a village of which Moncoutant is the lord. Moncoutant, Edrington, Hornblower and their men will disembark – with cannons –

Major Edrington (left), commander of the 'Lobsters' aiding the émigrés and (right), a 'Frog' in the shape of the Marquis de Moncoutant. Hornblower is the meat in a rather unpalatable sandwich.

and the former will rouse his loyal subjects into action against the Republican troops as well as holding a vital bridge and manning a ford in the event of enemy attack. Charette and the rest of the émigré forces disembark at nearby Quiberon where only the *Indy* is to remain at anchor in case the men have to retreat. But the *Indy* only has room for a quarter of the troops carried to France . . .

Moncoutant's reception in Muzillac is disastrous: the villagers are all Republicans now and clearly hate him. They refuse to lower the tricolour and, in his rage, Moncoutant kills the man who used to be the linen merchant and is now, to Moncoutant's horror, the mayor. The Englishmen are appalled. So is a young schoolteacher called Mariette who has already caught Hornblower's eye. Moncoutant has ordered the school to be closed and the children – 'peasants' – back to work in the fields. Hornblower, ever gallant, tries to defend Mariette from Moncoutant's more wounding remarks – and from the guillotine which is already chopping its way through insubordinate villagers.

Much has changed since Moncoutant was hounded out of France. His 'loyal' townspeople have turned Republican and Mariette has become Muzillac's first teacher. Moncoutant is determined to send Mariette and her charges 'back to the fields'. Mariette has an altogether different agenda . . .

All Moncoutant wants to do is execute recalcitrant villagers. His reluctant ally Hornblower is fast losing patience with the die-hard reactionary: and there are equally die-hard Republicans descending on Muzillac . . .

Pellew, meanwhile, has received a message from Charette's camp to the effect that the enemy is nowhere in sight. Pellew is worried rather than relieved. It's all too suspiciously quiet.

That changes at dawn the following day: the bridge at Muzillac is under attack. The attack is repulsed, but Edrington, at the nearby ford, is puzzled that the enemy have no artillery. That's because it is being used against Charette further west; Pellew's worst fears have been confirmed. The enemy decimates Charette's troops. Pellew sends a party ashore to try to make contact with them, but when they fail, Pellew has to assume that all the men have been killed. One of them is his own – Bowles. Pellew is distraught and deeply saddened that he was ordered to remain quiet about the stolen orders: it's quite clear that they fell into enemy hands.

Pellew takes the decision to return to Muzillac so that they will be on hand to rescue the party at the bridge should they also be repulsed. But the elements conspire against him: the wind fails and they are becalmed.

Edrington and Hornblower are having trouble with Moncoutant; he's their commanding officer but all he cares about is executing villagers. Hornblower, who is clearly smitten by Mariette – and vice versa, manages to elicit from her the information that Republican troops passed through the village three days previously. Hornblower and Edrington realize they are on their own. Then a cloud of dust in the distance turns out to be mounted Republican troops at the head of a column of infantry. Hornblower rides into Muzillac (he has rapidly, if imperfectly, learned to ride in this episode) and again tries to persuade Moncoutant to desist from killing his villagers and command his troops instead. Reluctantly, Moncoutant agrees.

Hornblower turns on Moncoutant, pleading with him to stop executing innocent people. Moncoutant is appalled by the insolence of the young lieutenant.

Now Hornblower is stuck with the émigrés in the village while Edrington, the Lobsters and Hornblower's men have formed a defence on the beach side of the Muzillac bridge. If they have to, they will blow up the bridge to protect themselves. And Hornblower is on the other side . . .

Meanwhile, Pellew has sent boats out from the becalmed *Indy*. Now he recalls them as, at last, a wind has arisen.

It's mayhem at Muzillac. The mob has turned on Moncoutant, dragging him to the guillotine. Hornblower realizes he has to escape – but he won't leave without Mariette. Pursued by Republican troops, they make it to the bridge just as his own men are about to blow it up, but Mariette is struck and killed by a Republican bullet. Hornblower is devastated and only under pressure from Kennedy does he cross the bridge to safety seconds before it is blown up.

Now they make an increasingly desperate stand on the beach. To everyone's surprise and relief, Bowles appears; he has escaped from the slaughter of Charette's men. But it looks as if no-one is going to escape the slaughter on the beach as the Republican troops surge across the river. And then the *Indy* appears, broadside to the beach, firing at the Republicans and forcing them to retreat.

The survivors return to the *Indy* and Pellew delivers words of wisdom – and admiration – to his favourite protégé.

This episode is based on chapter six of *Mr. Midshipman Hornblower* – which in turn was based on a 'real-life' Royalist landing at Quiberon on 20 July 1795. It ended, writes Forester 'in a disaster far worse than this one'.

While the action in the script is much the same as that in the book, the characters are much more fully developed. Mariette is barely mentioned – and certainly not as Hornblower's first love. Yet Andrew Benson is at pains to point out that creating this role for her was not simply a gratuitous nod to the exigencies of modern drama. True, it was deemed necessary to include romance in this series, but Andrew hopes that 'we've remained true to the spirit of the one romance that Forester did write about [with Barbara Wellesley, much later in Hornblower's career]. Everyone involved has read all the Hornblower books and we hope we've kept in character and reflected the sort of approach that Hornblower had at the beginning of that relationship. We certainly can't be accused of having made him a womanizer . . .'

Also, in the original book, Kennedy is mentioned only in passing, and though Edrington and Moncoutant exist, their essential characters are enlarged upon for the television series in order to provide greater contrast with each other. Moncoutant is actually an amalgam of two of Forester's characters, Moncoutant himself and the Marquis de Pouzauges. In the book, they are almost interchangeable; here, they work better as one.

Forester does not mention Charette, who actually existed. His endeavours to raise an army against the Republicans ended, as here, with his death.

(It's interesting to note that 'Frogs' is still an acceptable term of light-hearted abuse. Forester's dialogue is also sprinkled with references to the Spanish as 'damned dagoes'. Oddly enough, that phrase didn't make it into the scripts . . .)

Moncoutant gets his come-uppance. He was tempting fate by bringing a guillotine to France: the machine is about to do what it does best – chopping the heads off aristocrats.

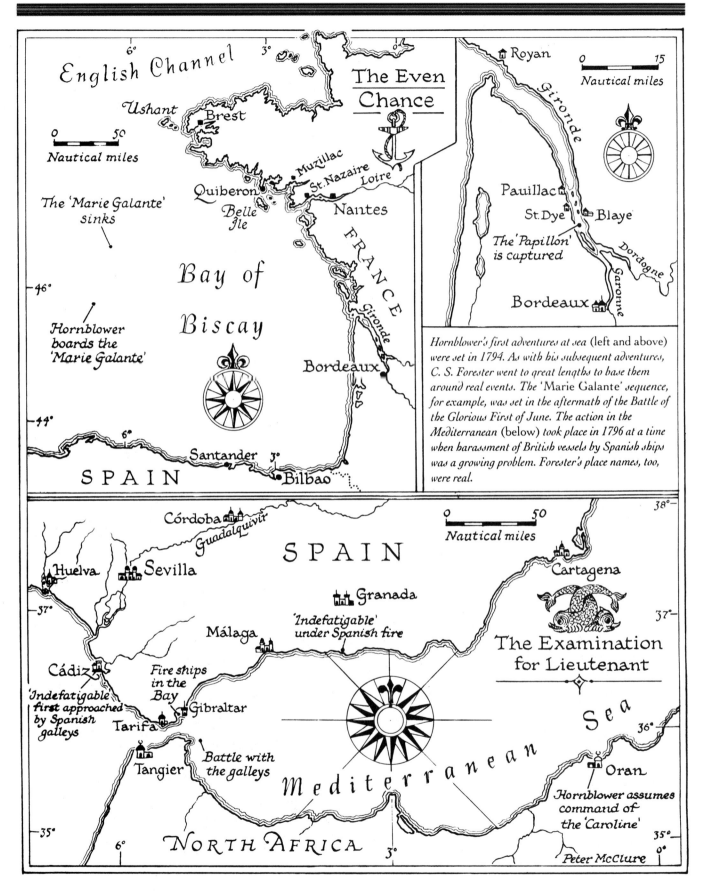

English Channel

6° 3° 0°

Ushant

Brest

Muzillac

St.Nazaire Loire

Quiberon

Belle Ile

Nantes

The Even Chance

Royan

Gironde

0 15
Nautical miles

Pauillac
St.Dye Blaye
The 'Papillon' is captured
Dordogne
Garonne
Bordeaux

The 'Marie Galante' sinks

0 50
Nautical miles

46°

Bay of

Hornblower boards the 'Marie Galante'

Biscay

FRANCE

Gironde

Bordeaux

44°

6° 3°

Santander

SPAIN Bilbao

Hornblower's first adventures at sea (left and above) were set in 1794. As with his subsequent adventures, C. S. Forester went to great lengths to base them around real events. The 'Marie Galante' sequence, for example, was set in the aftermath of the Battle of the Glorious First of June. The action in the Mediterranean (below) took place in 1796 at a time when harassment of British vessels by Spanish ships was a growing problem. Forester's place names, too, were real.

Córdoba
Guadalquivir

SPAIN

38°

Huelva Sevilla

0 50
Nautical miles

Cartagena

37°

Granada

'Indefatigable' under Spanish fire

Málaga

The Examination for Lieutenant

Cádiz

Fire ships in the Bay

'Indefatigable' first approached by Spanish galleys

Gibraltar

Tarifa

36°

Sea

Tangier

Battle with the galleys

Mediterranean

Oran

Hornblower assumes command of the 'Caroline'

35°

6°

NORTH AFRICA

3°

35°

0°

Peter McClure

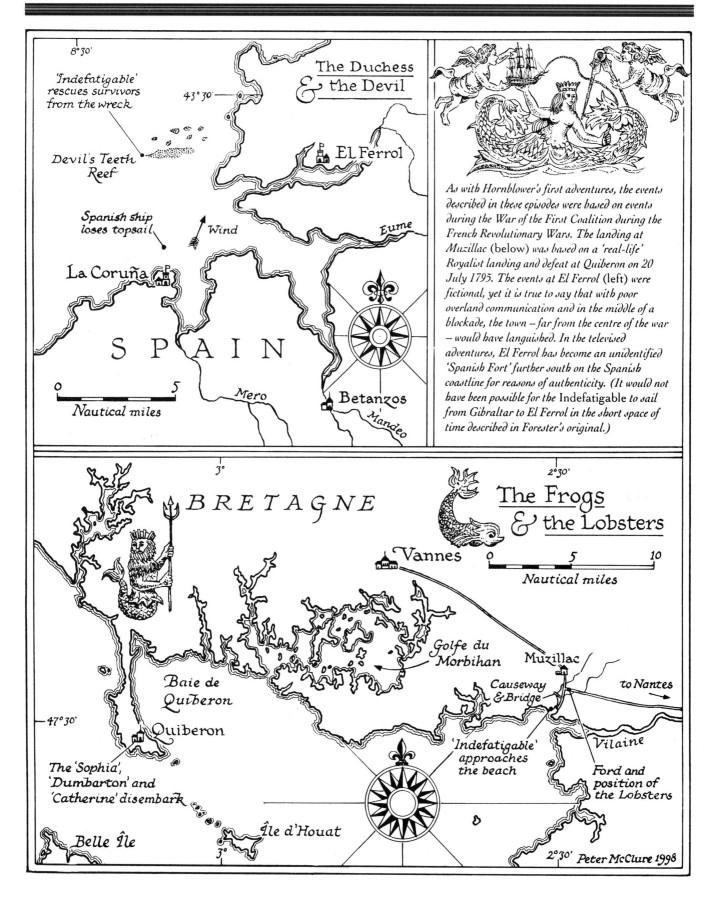

The Duchess & the Devil

'Indefatigable' rescues survivors from the wreck

Devil's Teeth Reef

Spanish ship loses topsail

La Coruña

8°30'

43°30'

El Ferrol

Eume

Wind

SPAIN

0 — 5
Nautical miles

Mero

Betanzos

Mandeo

As with Hornblower's first adventures, the events described in these episodes were based on events during the War of the First Coalition during the French Revolutionary Wars. The landing at Muzillac (below) was based on a 'real-life' Royalist landing and defeat at Quiberon on 20 July 1795. The events at El Ferrol (left) were fictional, yet it is true to say that with poor overland communication and in the middle of a blockade, the town — far from the centre of the war — would have languished. In the televised adventures, El Ferrol has become an unidentified 'Spanish Fort' further south on the Spanish coastline for reasons of authenticity. (It would not have been possible for the Indefatigable to sail from Gibraltar to El Ferrol in the short space of time described in Forester's original.)

BRETAGNE

The Frogs & the Lobsters

Vannes

0 — 5 — 10
Nautical miles

3°

2°30'

Golfe du Morbihan

Muzillac

Causeway & Bridge

to Nantes

Baie de Quiberon

47°30'

Quiberon

The 'Sophia', 'Dumbarton' and 'Catherine' disembark

Belle Île

Île d'Houat

3°

'Indefatigable' approaches the beach

Vilaine

Ford and position of the Lobsters

2°30' Peter McClure 1998

Glossary of Naval Terms (circa 1795)

Afterguard: Body of men working the aftersails from quarterdeck and poop.

Battery: (1) Section of a broadside commanded by a lieutenant or midshipman. (2) Gun position on land.

Beam: Widest part of a ship.

Between the Devil and the deep blue sea: The devil isn't Satan but the seam in the planking on the waterline. If a sailor found himself stuck there, he was in a pretty precarious position.

Bowsprit: Spar projecting over a ship's bow and spreading parts of the standing rigging and the jibs.

Brig: Two-masted, square-rigged vessel with a staysail on a boom on the aftermast.

Broadside: (1) The complete battery mounted on one side of a ship. (2) The simultaneous firing of all these guns.

Bulkhead: Vertical partition below decks.

Burgoo: A kind of porridge.

By and large: The expression dates from the days of square-rigged vessels. 'By the wind' meant that the wind was before the beam: 'sailing large' meant it was behind. 'By and large', therefore, implies a general balance between extremes.

Carronade: A short light cannon firing a disproportionately heavy ball at a low velocity.

Coxswain: Seaman in permanent charge of a ship's boat.

Cutter: (1) One-masted vessel rigged with a gaff mainsail, topsail, headsails and usually a square topsail. (2) Short ship's boat.

Davy Jones's Locker: Seamen's slang for the bottom of the sea. There are several theories as to the origin of the expression: one is that Davy Jones was the owner of a sixteenth-century London pub where unwary sailors were drugged and put in lockers, and then awoke aboard ship to find they had been press-ganged into the Navy.

In the doldrums: Being inactive or depressed – deriving from the doldrums near the equator where calm conditions prevail and sailing ships were often becalmed for days or weeks.

Flagship: Ship carrying an admiral, and therefore his flag.

Forecastle: Small deck built over the forward part of the main deck.

Foremast: Foremost of a ship's three masts.

Frigate: Fifth or Sixth 'rate' ship (ships were rated by the number of cannon they carried), most often with 32–38 cannon. Everyone but the captain lived on the unarmed 'gundeck' at the waterline.

Gaff: Spar extending the heads of certain fore-and-aft sails.

To run the gauntlet: Now meaning to go through an unpleasant experience, it derives from a naval and military punishment that became prominent during the Thirty Years War (1618–48), when an offender was forced to proceed between two lines of men who would attack him with clubs, whips or knotted cords. Derives from the Swedish 'gata', meaning road, and 'lopp', meaning course.

Heads: The crew's latrines, an open grating each side of the base of the bowsprit.

League: Three nautical miles.

Leeward: The direction towards which the wind is blowing.

Longboat: Largest of a ship's boats.

Maelstrom: Used to denote a confused turmoil, it was originally the name given to strong currents in the waters of Norway's Lofoten Islands. Derives from the Dutch 'malem' – to grind – and 'stroom', meaning stream.

Mainmast: Tallest mast, the central one of a ship.

Mast: (1) The complete foremast, mainmast or mizzenmast. (2) A section of these; as foremast, foretopmast, foretopgallant. Topmasts and topgallantmasts could be removed in heavy weather.

Mizzenmast: The aftermost (rear) mast of a ship or ketch.

Orlop: The lowest deck of a ship, lying above the hold and below the waterline.

Part of ship: One of a number of parties into which each watch was divided.

To take someone down a peg or two: Ships' flags were raised or lowered using pegs. To lower a flag meant to surrender . To 'nail your colours [flag] to the mast', on the other hand, is a declaration of firm allegiance and intent to carry on regardless.

Pinnace: Eight-oared ship's boat.

Plain sailing: Originally 'plane sailing', a simplified method of determining the course of a ship by assuming the earth is flat: lines of longitude and latitude are considered as perpendiculars. Accurate for short distances.

Poop: The highest aftermost deck of a ship, on the largest ships.

Privateer: Privately-owned ship of war, licensed by letter of marque (from the Lord High Admiral) to carry arms against a named enemy nation to her owners' profit.

Quarterdeck: Raised deck above the main deck; partly below the poop deck, if present. Often running half the length of a ship, it was reserved for officers.

Rating: (1) The station a person holds on the ship's books. (2) The rate of a ship. (3) Loosely, ordinary seamen.

No room to swing a cat: Denoting a cramped space, the expression is thought to derive from the days when a cat-o'-nine tails – a lash with nine knotted lines (hence a cat has nine lives) – was used to flog disobedient sailors. The punishment was carried out on deck as conditions below were too cramped. Other sources suggest that the 'cat' was originally a sailor's hammock or cot.

Royal: A square sail and mast above the topgallant.

Ship: Exclusively a square-rigged vessel with three (later, more) articulated masts.

Ships that pass in the night: 'Ships that pass in the night, and speak to each other in passing' – a line from 'Tales from a Wayside Inn' by US poet H. W. Longfellow (1807–82).

Ship-of-the-line: Also known as a line-of-battle ship. A man-of-war large enough to lie in the line of battle. By the 1790s, this meant in practice ships from the first to third rate.

Shipshape and Bristol fashion: Derives from the days when Bristol was a major trading port with a reputation for efficiency.

Sloop: (1) Any naval vessel commanded by a Commander, usually a small ship with 12–20 cannon. (2) A small, one-masted fore-and-aft vessel.

Spar: A length of timber, used in masting and rigging to spread sails.

Taffrail: The after-rail at a ship's stern.

Tender: An auxiliary vessel or boat.

Topgallant: The mast and sails above the topmast, itself above the mainmast on an articulated mast.

Topman: A seaman who works aloft.

Wardroom: Lieutenants' and warrant officers' mess. In a frigate it was aft, on the waterline, below the captain's cabin.

Watch: (1) One of the seven divisions of the nautical day. (2) One of the two or three divisions into which seamen were divided for work and leisure.

To take the wind out of someone's sails: If a square-rigged ship sailed too close to another on the windward side, it would deprive the latter of wind and therefore the power to move.

Yard: A long spar across a mast to support and spread a sail.

Windward: The direction from which the wind is blowing.

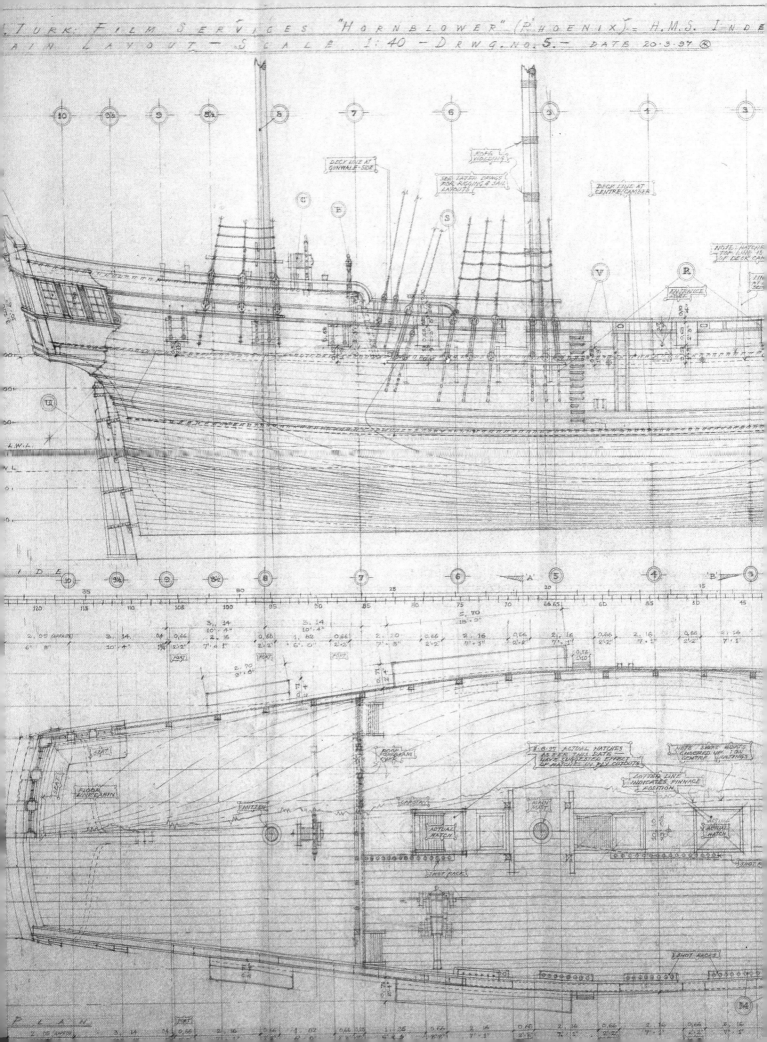

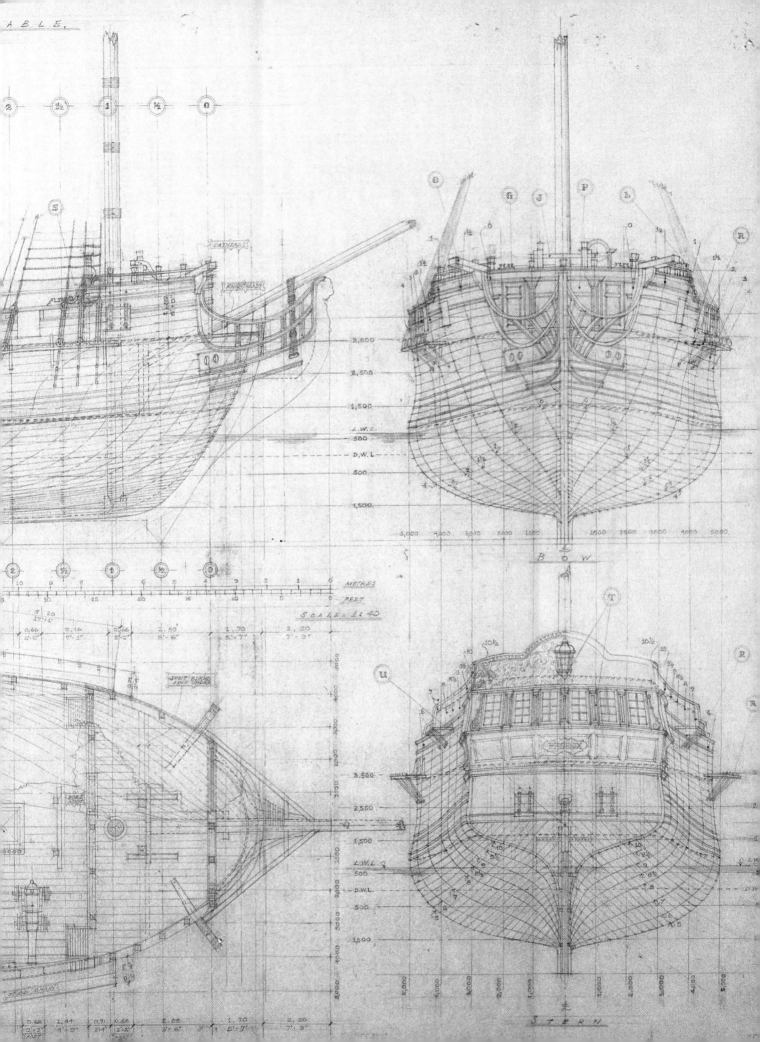